PINK!

Stacy Davidowitz

D1552484

BROADWAY PLAY PUBLISHING INC
224 E 62nd St, NY NY 10065-8201
212 772-8334 fax: 212 772-8358
BroadwayPlayPubl.com

PINK!
© Copyright 2011 by Stacy Davidowitz

First printing July 2011
I S B N: 978-0-88145-474-1

Book design: Marie Donovan
Page make-up: Adobe Indesign
Typeface: Palatino
Printed and bound in the U S A

ABOUT THE AUTHOR

Stacy Davidowitz is a playwright and actor who has had work developed and produced in New York City, Chicago, Boston, and Los Angeles. PINK! was a 2009 Lark Play Development Center Playwrights' Week Finalist and received seven New York Innovative Theater Nominations, including Outstanding Full Length Script, for its production by Down Payment Productions at the WorkShop Theater, N Y C. Her screenplay of PINK! is currently being optioned as an independent feature film. Her children's musical HANK & GRETCHEN: A MODERN RE-TELLING OF HANSEL & GRETEL; OR BECAUSE CANDY IS THAT GOOD was produced with a cast of 54 fifth graders in N Y, June 2011. Her full-length play THE RUBBER ROOM is currently in development with Down Payment Productions, and her play RUN. RUN. STOP. will be produced as part of the 36th Annual Samuel French Off Off Broadway Short Play Festival in July 2011. A recipient of the Bob Hope Endowed Fellowship, Stacy is a graduate of British American Drama Academy; B S, Tufts University; M F A in Acting, Columbia University. www.StacyDavidowitz. com

PINK! was first produced by Down Payment
Productions (Jessica Fisch, Artistic Director; Executive
Producer, Brian Smith; Alec Strum, Associate Artistic
Director; Emily Kent, General Manager) opening on
10 September 2009 at the WorkShop Theater in New
York City. The cast and creative contributors were:

ASHLEY	Caitlin Mehner
ZOE	Kaela Crawford
TRACY	Alison Scaramella
SAMANTHA	Julia Giolzetti
ABBY	Stephanie Strohm
Director	Brian Smith
Set designer	Amanda Stephens
Costume designer	Stephanie Alexander
Lighting designer	Joel Silver
Dramaturg	Alec Strum
Production stage manager	Johanna Thelin
Assistant stage manager	Kaitlin Del Campo
Production manager	Matthew Saide
Wed video designer	Laura Willcox

CHARACTERS

(In order of SUPERIORITY)

ASHLEY, *queen of the bunk, controlling, manipulative, intelligent, experienced beyond her years, 12*

ZOE, *popular by association, immature, inexperienced, underdeveloped, insensitive,* ASHLEY's *pet, 12*

TRACY, *camp clown, effortlessly beautiful, takes charge, impulsive, potty mouth, 12*

SAMANTHA, *new camper, quietly judgmental observer, journal-writer, 12*

ABBY, *eager to be popular, victimized, jealous, chubby, delusional concerning her social status, 12*

Actors over the age of 18 should be playing these characters, not 12 year-old girls—unless you want to get sued.

If the run is longer than 90 minutes…you're fucking it up.

A FEW NOTES

I LOVE camp. In fact, I am obsessed with it. I am obsessed with it in the same way that all people are obsessed with their camp, but more. It is my favorite place in the world.

None of the characters and events of PINK! are based on real people and events. This play is entirely fictional. Thank God.

I'd like to thank Brian Smith for his brilliance and ambition, and my incredibly supportive family and friends for making me a very, very happy person.

Enjoy.

(An upscale, air-conditioned summer sleep-away camp cabin. Night. 2009. Tie-dyed quilts, Build-A-Bears, Jonas Brothers posters, pictures of grandparents, parents, and home friends, jacks, pink stationary, floral designs, flashlights, Mad Libs, diaries, opened mail, overflowing garbage bin with Cup O' Noodles, candy wrappers, dirty laundry, iPods, D S Guitar Hero. Very 12. They are 12. Lights up. ASHLEY, with Japanese straightened hair, bronzer, and clear braces; ZOE, petite and ratty; TRACY, effortlessly beautiful and sporty; SAMANTHA, frumpy in her unique and poor choice of style; and ABBY, bloated with baby fat, insecurity, and unlimited, eager energy, burst into the bunk screaming, jumping, dancing, laughing, humping, drunk with excitement. The bunk is their jungle gym, and their energy is unleashed, wild, insane, and irresistibly contagious. Their lines preceding the dance are right on top of each other, often overlapping.)

TRACY: We won beyotches!

ASHLEY/ZOE: We won! We won!

ABBY: Oh my god, we won!

SAMANTHA: We actually did it!

TRACY: Oh yeah! Oh yeah!

ABBY: We did it!

TRACY: Talent show geniuses!

ZOE: We are the bestest best!

ASHLEY: Oh my god, you are so cute!

TRACY: Talent show! Uh!

ABBY/ASHLEY/SAMANTHA/TRACY/ZOE: (*Cheering*)
Talent show! Uh! We won!
Talent show! Uh! We won!
Talent show! Uh! We won!

(*The girls break into a pre-rehearsed group cheer specific to their bunk.*)

SAMANTHA: I can't believe we got first place!

ABBY: Duh, we got first place!

ZOE: We beat like all the other girls!

TRACY: Upper and lower camp, beyotches!

ASHLEY: Fuck yeah!

ABBY: Like the little kids always win cause they're cute!

ZOE: But we're cuter now!

SAMANTHA: And we beat the Seniors!

ASHLEY: They were like what the fuck?

TRACY: I know!

ZOE: I saw Ryan stare at Ashley!

ABBY: They were ALL looking at her cause she's so pretty!

TRACY: I was like one, two, three, uh. Five, six, seven, uh.

SAMANTHA: You were so good!

ZOE: Like the sexiest sexy!

TRACY: We were all amazing. I'm just the *choreo*-grapher.

ABBY: Ash, you were so good when you did the body roll thing!

SAMANTHA: Have you guys ever won before?

ABBY: It's like really hard, Samantha.

SAMANTHA: I was just asking.

TRACY: See? When you put in a little bit of effort and stuff it pays off.

ZOE: Remember when I did my walk and everyone was like oh my god!

ASHLEY: So sexy!

TRACY: I'm like drunk off of being sexy.

ZOE: Sexy, sexy, sexy!

TRACY: Vagina! We're doing the dance.

ZOE: The boys are probably gonna watch through the window.

ASHLEY: They're probably gonna watch you cause you're so cute!

ABBY: And you, Ash!

ASHLEY: Shut up.

TRACY: Somebody put the music on!

ABBY/ASHLEY/SAMANTHA/TRACY/ZOE: Shot not!

ZOE: Abby, you do it.

ABBY: I don't want to be the one who just like presses play.

SAMANTHA: Do it. Oh my god.

ASHLEY: Oh my god, please, Abby.

TRACY: Join after you start the music.

ABBY: Fine, fine.

TRACY: In front of the mirror.

ZOE: Press it!

ABBY: I'm finding it.

ASHLEY: Forget it. I'm not dancing.

SAMANTHA: Come on, Abby!

TRACY: Ash, please, we need you.

ASHLEY: Fine. Abby, stop being a retard!

TRACY: Vagina! Positions!

ABBY: Get your freak on!

ASHLEY: What?

TRACY: O K, arms, arms.

(ABBY *goes to the iPod pre-set in the iPod speaker and plays* Womanizer *by Britney Spears. Or* Kosher Boy (Crack Dat) *by Eric Schwartz, parody of* Crank That *by Soulja Boy. Or* Just Dance *by Lady Gaga. Or* I Kissed A Girl *by Katy Perry. The girls get into their positions, a sort of V with* TRACY *in the front,* ASHLEY *and* ZOE *on either side of her in the next row, and* ABBY *and* SAMANTHA *in the back. They do the choreographed dance they won the talent show with earlier that night. After the choreographed part is over, the girls break into an exhilarating, ridiculous dance party.* ABBY *and* SAMANTHA *fight. Physically.* ABBY *falls to the floor, holding her ankle. Party's over.*)

ABBY: Ow, ow, ow.

TRACY: What's the problem?

ABBY: Samantha tripped me and I sprained my ankle again!

ASHLEY: Seriously?

SAMANTHA: I didn't do anything!

(SAMANTHA *turns the music off.* TRACY *helps* ABBY *off of the floor.*)

ABBY: Ow, it hurts!

ASHLEY: Oh my god.

ZOE: She always ruins everything.

(ASHLEY *goes to her bed, lounging like a queen, and then sits up to make room for* ZOE's *head in her lap.* ASHLEY *plays with* ZOE *like she's her pet.* ZOE *is her pet.* SAMANTHA *returns to her bed and is immediately engrossed in her book,* You Are So Not Invited To My Bat Mitzvah. TRACY *tries to help* ABBY *to her bed.*)

ABBY: No, I can't make it that far. Zoe's bed is closer.

(TRACY *helps* ABBY *to* ZOE's *bed.*)

ZOE: Ew.

TRACY: O K, point your toe. Like this.

ABBY: Ow!

ZOE: She's such a faker.

TRACY: O K, roll your ankle like this.

ABBY: Shhhahhhhooww.

ASHLEY: I think they might have to amputate it.

SAMANTHA: Looks like you won't be able to dance for a while.

ABBY: It's your fault I got hurt, Samantha.

TRACY: No one's punishing you for getting hurt. You just can't physically dance now.

(ASHLEY *plays with* ZOE's *camera and takes an unflattering picture of* ABBY *who pretends not to notice.*)

ABBY: Well, you don't have to show off and like brag about it.

TRACY: What?

ZOE: She isn't!

SAMANTHA: What does that even mean?

(ASHLEY *takes another unflattering picture of* ABBY.)

ZOE: Yeah, what are you talking about? (*Silence*) Hello?

ABBY: I can dance if I feel better. Like if I want to.

ZOE: You would just break your other ankle.

SAMANTHA: It's a sprain.

ABBY: That's stupid.

TRACY: Fine, everything that you're not involved in is stupid.

ABBY: That's not what I said.

(ASHLEY *takes another picture of* ABBY.)

TRACY: That's what you're thinking.

SAMANTHA: Tracy is obviously the best person to teach the dance.

ZOE: Stop being so jealous of her.

ABBY: I'm not.

SAMANTHA: You are.

ABBY: *(To* ASHLEY*)* What are you doing?

ZOE: It's so obvious.

ABBY: *(To* ZOE*)* No, it's not.

(ASHLEY *takes another picture of* ABBY.)

ZOE: Jellyfish jello jealous!

(*The girls laugh with the exception of* ABBY.)

TRACY: Whatever, who cares. All this dancing makes me have to shit.

(*All the girls laugh hysterically as* TRACY *runs to the bathroom to take a shit.* ASHLEY *takes another picture of* ABBY.)

ABBY: Ash, what're you—

ASHLEY: FUCK ME!

ABBY/SAMANTHA/ZOE: What???

ASHLEY: So, basically no one understands me. No one.

ZOE: I understand you.

ASHLEY: Aw. You're so cute.

ABBY: I understand you.

ASHLEY: No you don't.

TRACY: Vagina!

ZOE: Ha! Vagina!

TRACY/ZOE: One, two, three… Vagina! Jinx!

SAMANTHA: Shh.

ABBY: Vagina!

ASHLEY: Get out of my personal space.

TRACY: Vagina *ata adonai elohenu melech ha olam*—

SAMANTHA: Seriously, can you please be quiet?

TRACY: Shit. Shit. Shit!

ZOE: She's practicing her *haftorah*. And she has to work on it or else she can't have a party. Right?

TRACY: Vagina!

ZOE: Right.

ABBY: When's your Bat Mitzvah again, Tracy?

ASHLEY: You weren't invited?

ABBY: I was invited.

ASHLEY: So, why don't you know when it is?

ABBY: I forgot. Jesus.

ASHLEY: You forgot Jesus?

TRACY: Vagina!

ZOE: She should forget Jesus. She's getting Bat Mitzvahed! Get it? She's Jewish so she shouldn't believe—

ASHLEY: Oh my god, Zoe. You are so funny.

(ASHLEY *and* ZOE *laugh hysterically.* ABBY *joins.* ASHLEY *and* ZOE *stop laughing.* ABBY *laughs by herself and then stops.* SAMANTHA *laughs at* ABBY.)

TRACY: Ow!

ABBY: Are you ok?

TRACY: Shitty shit shit!

ZOE: O K, I'm coming to help!

TRACY: No, stop, don't come in.

ABBY: Tracy's like dying.

TRACY: I feel like I'm pooping out a baby!

ZOE: Should I get Christy?

SAMANTHA: That is so disgusting. Can you guys stop?

TRACY: No counselors! It's just a big poop.

ABBY: She's having a baby!

ASHLEY: Go take your Ritilin, Abby.

ABBY: I don't take it at camp.

ASHLEY: Spare us all and take it.

TRACY: Shitty shit shit!

SAMANTHA: Ew. I need to brush my teeth in there before bed.

TRACY: O K, I'm almost done!

SAMANTHA: It smells.

ZOE: Tracy needs our moral support. Are you not supporting her?

SAMANTHA: Always and forever I support you, Tracy.

TRACY: Thanks, Sammi.

SAMANTHA: That's not my name.

ASHLEY: It's *Samantha*.

ZOE: Why can't we call you Sammi? It's so cute!

ASHLEY: If your name were *Samantha*, we'd call you Sammi, Zoe. But *Samantha* doesn't have that same cuteness so it makes sense that we'd call her *Samantha*. No offense.

(TRACY *enters from the bathroom*.)

SAMANTHA: None taken.

ABBY: Yeah, cause you're so cute, Zoe.

ZOE: *(Overlapping with ASHLEY)* Thanks.

ASHLEY: *(Overlapping with ZOE)* Shut up.

ZOE: Fuck me!

ASHLEY: Oh my god, you are so innocent! I LOVE you, Zoe!

ABBY: You love her? Like love love?

ASHLEY: Shut the fuck up. And yes, I love you, Zoe!

ZOE: I love you!

TRACY: Make out!

SAMANTHA: At least do it in private. Please.

ABBY: You don't have to watch.

TRACY: With tongue!

ABBY: They're gonna do it!

ZOE: Ew, Abby, you're so gross.

ASHLEY: Just ignore, Zoe. Just ignore.

ABBY: Tracy, when is your Bat Mitzvah again?

ASHLEY: You already asked her that!

ZOE: Stop being extra annoying today.

ASHLEY: Everyone is really pissing me off.

ZOE: Pissing. Yellow piss!

ASHLEY: Zoe, you are so random!

ABBY: Fine. Forget it. I refuse to talk.

TRACY: When is my Bat Mitzvah you ask? When is my Bat Mitzvah? Ladies and Gentlemen, the most exciting day of your life when I will be a woman like no woman has been a womanly woman before is…drum roll, please…

ABBY: Boom, boom, boom.

ASHLEY: What the fuck is that supposed to be?

ZOE: Boom, boom, boom!

ASHLEY: Hilarious.

TRACY: Boom, boom, boom, boom. I want you in my room, to spend the night together—

ZOE: You're saying the words to that song!

TRACY/ZOE: (*Singing*) Boom, boom, boom, boom. I want you in my room, to spend the night together, together in my room! Boom, boom—

ABBY: Whatever, I don't care anymore.

TRACY: O K, O K, the best date in the whole wide, wide, wide world is…September—please don't do the drum roll, Abby—

ABBY: I'm not!

TRACY: Twenty-fifth!

ABBY: Oh, yeah!

ZOE: Why are you even asking?

ABBY: I'm writing all the dates in my new planner and I forgot to write Tracy's down. Is that O K with you?

SAMANTHA: That's my date.

TRACY: What?

ASHLEY: Oh, shit. Fight's on.

TRACY: Are you serious?

SAMANTHA: Yeah.

TRACY: Why didn't you say anything?

SAMANTHA: Obviously, I didn't know.

ZOE: Well, are we even invited?

SAMANTHA: What is that supposed to mean?

ASHLEY: Are we invited? Simple.

SAMANTHA: Obviously.

ASHLEY: Well, we don't have invitations. So, not that obvious.

ZOE: I've never not been invited to a friend's Bat Mitzvah.

ABBY: How do you know? Maybe you just never found out.

ZOE: Doubt it.

ASHLEY: Once again, ignore.

SAMANTHA: I didn't know you guys before the summer, but now that I know you, I'll give you your invitations late.

ZOE: You knew Abby.

ASHLEY: Did you invite her?

SAMANTHA: Yeah.

ASHLEY: Cause that would be pretty mean if you didn't. Just saying.

ZOE: Yeah, you like knew each other since you were babies. And now, you're gonna be family!

ABBY: Ew. Don't say that!

TRACY: Abby!

ABBY: I wish I didn't even get her ugly invitation.

ASHLEY: What does it look like?

ABBY: Oh my god, Ashley, it's so funny!

TRACY: Don't be mean, Abby.

ABBY: Oh my god, it's a C D with a picture of her face on it!

SAMANTHA: Shut up!

ZOE: What do you mean?

ABBY: It has her like singing her invitation out loud.

ASHLEY: Are you serious?

ZOE: Really?

SAMANTHA: It was my mom's idea.

ASHLEY: That is hilarious.

ABBY: It's so funny.

TRACY: Can we hear it?

ZOE: I want to hear it! I want to hear it!

ASHLEY: Get it, Abby.

SAMANTHA: No.

TRACY: Hi, family and friends! I'm Sam!

ASHLEY: *Samantha!*

TRACY: *(Singing obnoxiously)* And this is my Bat Mitzvah invitation!

ASHLEY: Play it!

TRACY: *(Singing)* It is on September 25th!

ABBY: Give me your invitation, Samantha.

SAMANTHA: No.

ASHLEY/ZOE: Yes!

TRACY: *(Singing)* I have the same date as the world famous Tracy so no one—

SAMANTHA: I don't have it, anyway.

TRACY: *(Singing)* You're interrupting my singing! So no one will go—

ZOE: Abby, where's yours?

TRACY: *(Singing)* To mine!

ABBY: You actually think I'd waste space in my duffle to bring that?

ZOE: A C D takes up no space.

TRACY: *(Singing)* I'm crying so hard! Boo-hoo! La la la!

ASHLEY: Forget it. You're useless.

ABBY: No, I mean, I can ask my mom to send it up or something.

ASHLEY: You blow.

TRACY: *(Singing)* Abby blows!

ABBY: You blow, Ash! Haha! Get it? Like blow-jo—

ASHLEY: Stop saying my name like we're friends.

ZOE: You guys as friends equals so five years ago.

ASHLEY: Zoe, that was one of the funniest things you've ever said!

ZOE: Yay! I'm funny!

ASHLEY: Stop it, you're so cute! Samantha, I still want an invitation.

SAMANTHA: I already said you're invited, so you'll all get them. Happy?

ASHLEY: When?

ZOE: I want mine now!

ASHLEY: Write to your mom now and tell her to send the invitations to us at camp so we can be sure we're invited.

TRACY: Does anyone else see the real issue here? Samantha and I have the same date. And I live in Florida. So figure that one out, beyotches.

SAMANTHA: Don't say that.

ABBY: So…

TRACY: So…

ASHLEY: Vote!

ZOE: Yay! Vote!

SAMANTHA: Forget it, don't go to mine.

TRACY: Samantha…

SAMANTHA: No, it's fine.

ASHLEY: You're not fine, Samantha.

ZOE: Nope.

ASHLEY: So, we're gonna vote.

ABBY: I don't want to vote.

ASHLEY: Cause you want to go to Florida or you don't want to go to Florida?

ABBY: I don't want to vote.

ASHLEY: O K, blind vote.

ABBY: I don't want to do a blind vote either.

ASHLEY: O K, everyone close your eyes.

ABBY: I said, I don't think we should.

ASHLEY: Samantha, eyes. Shut. Tracy?

TRACY: They're shut.

ASHLEY: O K, raise your hand if you plan on going to Tracy's Bat Mitzvah.

(TRACY *raises both her hands ecstatically.* ZOE *raises her hand.* ABBY *abstains. Obviously, so does* SAMANTHA.)

ASHLEY: ABBY, you suck and aren't voting. Raise your hand now for Samantha's Bat Mitzvah extravaganza.

(*No one votes.*)

SAMANTHA: It's not going to be an extravaganza. It's going to be simple.

ZOE: Boring.

TRACY: It'll probably be classy is what she means.

ASHLEY: Yeah, way to sell it, Samantha. Now who wants to go to Samantha's?

ZOE: My mom said I'm having like a real trained monkey hand out the place cards.

ABBY: Oh, I've heard about that monkey!

ZOE: No, you haven't. It's original.

ABBY: I'm pretty sure—

ASHLEY: If she says it's original, then it is.

ZOE: I'm not lying!

ASHLEY: Abby, you can open your eyes.

ABBY: Oh. Oops.

TRACY: My centerpieces are going to be chocolate sculptures of my face.

ABBY: How are you not going to eat them at your party?

ASHLEY: Tracy isn't A D D. Or fat.

ABBY: My best friend from home is having Clay Aiken sing at her Bat Mitzvah cause her dad knows someone who works for *American Idol*.

ASHLEY: Gay.

TRACY: What's your give-away going to be?

ZOE: We're giving away candles in the shape of a Z.

ABBY: That's so creative.

ZOE: Um, I was obviously kidding. I'm giving away *Tiffany* dog tags.

TRACY: Seriously?

ZOE: Yeah.

ABBY: Woof!

ASHLEY: Grow up.

ABBY: I am growing up! I'm giving away *Brookstone* alarm clocks that have my date written on them. Every day the alarm goes off, I grow more!

ZOE: My mom wakes me up in the morning.

ASHLEY: Yeah, no one needs that.

TRACY: What about you, Ash?

ASHLEY: *Nano.*

TRACY: Sweet!

ABBY: You already told me that!

ASHLEY: Why would I ever tell you anything?

TRACY: The new one?

ASHLEY: No, the old one. Duh, the new one.

ZOE: Obvi.

ABBY: That would have gone perfect with my back up give away. It's this teddy bear but inside it's really an *iPod* speaker!

TRACY: Cool!

ASHLEY: Creepy.

ZOE: Tracy, what's yours?

TRACY: Oh my, oh my. The adults are gonna LOVE it! They get gym membership if they live in my town.

ZOE: Who cares? What about us?

TRACY: We get…

ABBY: Boyfriends!

ASHLEY: Someone punch her.

ZOE: Fruit punch! Pow!

ASHLEY: Oh my god. Hilarious.

TRACY: We get the best, the craziest, the bop bop bop to the top…

ZOE: Say it! I'm so excited!

TRACY: We cracked out kids get…Abby, drum roll…

ABBY: No.

TRACY: And the crowd goes wild over…T-shirts!

(ABBY, ASHLEY, *and* ZOE *laugh hysterically while* TRACY *says her line.*)

TRACY: I'm just kidding! I'm just kidding! Jokes! L O L!

ZOE: I believed you!

ABBY: I felt so bad for you for like a second!

TRACY: O K, ladies and gentle-women, you will all soon receive…a…ca…ca…cam…

ZOE: Say it!

TRACY: Camera!

ABBY/ASHLEY/ZOE: Yay!

ZOE: Amazing!

ABBY: That's the best give-away ever!

ASHLEY: Digital or throw away?

TRACY: The new *Canon* one. S D something.

ZOE: I already have a new camera.

ABBY: Samantha, what about you?

SAMANTHA: I don't know yet.

ABBY: What do you mean you don't know yet?

SAMANTHA: I mean, I don't know.

ASHLEY: Your Bat Mitzvah is basically right after camp.

ZOE: You have to order the give-aways like years ahead.

ASHLEY: Months, not years.

TRACY: Maybe it's flowers or something.

ABBY: It's not a funeral. Wait, it's not pajama pants, is it?

ASHLEY: It's probably T-shirts.

ZOE: Oh my god, is it?

ABBY: Is it?

ZOE: Wait, really?

ASHLEY: It's T-shirts.

ABBY: Oh my god! That's so funny!

ASHLEY: Why is that funny?

ABBY: Cause, I don't know.

ZOE: Wait, is anyone going to Samantha's?

TRACY: Who won the vote?

ABBY: We should all just figure it out on our own. And not talk about it.

ZOE: I'm going to Tracy's, no offense. I already have my flight booked.

ASHLEY: O K, raise your hand if you already have your flight booked to Florida.

(ZOE *raises her hand.*)

ASHLEY: Hello? O K, that's me and Zoe. Fine, Abby, be annoying and don't vote.

ZOE: We're going to Florida!

ASHLEY: Zoe, you know you're sitting next to me on the plane, right?

ZOE: No!

ASHLEY: Your mom didn't tell you?

ZOE: No!

ASHLEY: Yup!

ZOE: We're flying together! Yay!

ASHLEY: Oh my god, you're so cute.

SAMANTHA: Congratulations, everyone.

TRACY: Now I feel bad.

ZOE: Yeah, I feel really bad.

ABBY: You can't be mad at me cause I didn't vote.

ASHLEY: You didn't vote cause you *have* to go to Samantha's.

ZOE: It doesn't count for being nice if you like have to go.

SAMANTHA: I don't care if she goes or not.

ABBY: Why would I want to go? Ew.

ZOE: Haha! Your parents are like doing it.

ASHLEY: Oh my god, Zoe!

ZOE: Oops.

ASHLEY: Whatever, it's true.

TRACY: Can you change the date?

SAMANTHA: Don't flatter yourself. I wouldn't change the date for you.

ASHLEY: Oooh, things are getting heated.

SAMANTHA: Just…just stop.

ASHLEY: Samantha…

SAMANTHA: Don't interrupt me. I'm reading.

TRACY: I'm so sorry. I still feel really bad.

ASHLEY: Wait, that's so funny. Look at the title of her book.

ZOE: *You Are So Not Invited To My Bat Mitzvah!*

ASHLEY/ZOE: You are so not invited to my Bat Mitzvah!

SAMANTHA: Wow, you can read!

ASHLEY/ZOE: Wow, you can read!

ABBY: Wow, you can—

TRACY: I'm calling a Bunk Fourteen's Feelings.

ABBY: No!

TRACY: Yes. We all need it.

ASHLEY: Fine, but I'm mediator.

TRACY: No, you were mediator last time and people cried.

ZOE: That's so mean, Tracy. Also, you weren't crying, so you shouldn't care.

ABBY: Just let her do it, Tracy. She wants to.

TRACY: Seriously? Fine, it wasn't me sobbing.

ABBY: I'm sitting outside on the porch.

ASHLEY: No, you're not.

ABBY: The counselors all said I don't have to do it.

TRACY: How are we supposed to work together as a bunk if we're not all here?

ABBY: Not all of us ARE here! Dani's home for that family reunion, Riley is at the Health Center—

ZOE: Wait, does she have lice?

ASHLEY: I'll kill her if she does.

TRACY: She doesn't. And that's mean to say.

ASHLEY: Then what is it?

TRACY: I don't know, like a headache or something.

SAMANTHA: She's throwing up. She's staying there all night.

ASHLEY: Ew.

ZOE: Abby, it doesn't matter. You're here now so you have to be here now for this here!

ABBY: What?

TRACY: Plus, we all have things we want to say to each other.

ASHLEY: Too bad, Abby.

TRACY: If you don't listen, then nothing's going to be fixed.

ZOE: You just can't not be at the bunk meeting.

ABBY: O K! Fine!

ASHLEY: Are you going to cry again too?

ABBY: No.

TRACY: Shot not telling Christy.

ABBY/SAMANTHA/ZOE: Shot not!

ABBY: Ashley has to do it! She didn't say it!

ASHLEY: You actually think I'm getting up?

ABBY: You have to tell Christy that we need time alone for the meeting.

ASHLEY: That's a joke.

ZOE: You do it, Abby.

ABBY: Why me?

ASHLEY: Thanks so much, Abby.

ABBY: I'm not doing it. She's talking to her boyfriend and it's awkward.

ZOE: Yeah, thanks.

ASHLEY: It's so sweet of you. So, tell her she'll ruin everything if she comes in.

ZOE: Tell her we could like get her fired for talking to her boyfriend when she's supposed to be like taking care of us.

TRACY: No, cause then she'll come back in.

ZOE: Tell her we pay her salary so we're like her bosses and we say she can't come in.

TRACY: Forget it. I'll go. (*She goes out to the porch.*)

ASHLEY: Rude. You just made Tracy go cause you're too lazy.

ZOE: And scared.

ASHLEY: And annoying.

ABBY: You should have gone.

ASHLEY: Riiight.

ZOE: She meant, "yeah right!"

ASHLEY: Oh my god, Zoe, I like want to eat you up right now. You are so cute!

ZOE: Don't eat me up!

ASHLEY: Then stop saying hilarious things!

(TRACY *enters from the porch.*)

TRACY: O K, Christy "respects" us so we're good for like at least…

ASHLEY: An hour?

TRACY: However long until we're done and someone gets her I guess. O K, let's start. Everyone on your own beds.

ZOE: Why?

TRACY: Those are the rules.

ASHLEY: Zoe needs to be on my bed. O K, I'll start.

TRACY: Ash, just don't like phrase things how you phrased them last time.

ASHLEY: I will be very, very, very sensitive. Promise. Lights out.

ABBY: I hate the lights out.

ASHLEY: And I hate you so shh…

TRACY: Not nice.

ASHLEY: Sorry. Just kidding, you're my best friend. O K, everyone has to say something personal or a confession or what's bothering them. You can take out your personal lists and a pen if you want. No interruptions, no responding, no laughing. Lights out, I said!

(The girls take out their personal lists—camp stationary prepared with grievances against their bunkmates. They will refer to their lists throughout Bunk Fourteen's Feelings. SAMANTHA uses her journal. She observes and writes throughout the rest of the night.)

ZOE: Lights out!

SAMANTHA: Stop copying whatever Ashley says. *(She turns the lights off.)*

ZOE: What?

ASHLEY: That is rude.

TRACY: Vagina, we're starting!

ASHLEY: Let's start with…

ZOE: Abby, do your drum roll!

ABBY: No.

ASHLEY: Please?

ABBY: No.

ASHLEY: Please, please, please?

ABBY: Fine. Boom, boom—

ASHLEY: I was kidding. O K, let's start with…

ZOE: Me!

ASHLEY: Zoe.

ZOE: Yay! O K, O K. So…Abby.

ABBY: What?

ZOE: So…Abby.

ABBY: What?

ZOE: So…Abby.

ABBY: WHAT?

ZOE: I feel like you're always touching me and stuff. I know you really like me and like standing over me and like hanging out with me and Ashley, but it makes me feel uncomfortable when you touch me, like hug me and stuff. It's awkward. *(Pause)* So…are you going to respond?

ABBY: We're not supposed to respond.

ZOE: Oh. But can you?

TRACY: Moving on.

ZOE: I'm just curious like what you want to say to that.

ASHLEY: Me too. *(Silence)* But she obviously has no response—

ABBY: Well, Ashley doesn't mind cause she tells me stuff. Personal stuff—

ASHLEY: No, I don't!

TRACY: You tell her stuff?

ZOE: What stuff?

TRACY: What do you tell her?

ABBY: We talk about—

ASHLEY: Next!

ABBY: Things that best friends—

ASHLEY: You are NOT my best friend. Next!

ABBY: I'll go.

ASHLEY: No.

TRACY: You want to go?

ASHLEY: Oh my god.

ABBY: I don't know.

ASHLEY: What do you mean you don't know?

ABBY: I don't have anything to say.

ASHLEY: Then why do you want to go?

TRACY: Try to think of something.

ABBY: My ankle hurts? I don't know.

ASHLEY: You failed. That is neither personal nor interesting nor a confession.

TRACY: It's kind of a confession.

ASHLEY: It's not a confession if she hops around all day complaining.

TRACY: True. What else?

ABBY: Um, I don't know.

TRACY: Oh my god, I'm trying to be nice, but this doesn't count as participating in the meeting.

ASHLEY: This is just unproductive.

ABBY: I don't know what to say.

ASHLEY: If you won't speak for yourself, I'll speak for you.

ABBY: No, I don't want—

ASHLEY: Confession numero uno.

ZOE: That means number one!

SAMANTHA: Duh.

ZOE: Rude.

ASHLEY: So, I'm Abby right now. And, as Abby, I want to admit to everyone in the bunk that I've been stealing Ashley's things.

ABBY: What?

ASHLEY: I won't say another thing about it.

TRACY: What are you talking about?

ZOE: She did! I saw her take Ashley's headphones.

ABBY: They're mine!

TRACY: Are you stealing now too?

ABBY: No!

ZOE: Ashley said that they were hers cause there was a crack on the top. And I remember when she sat on them on the bus on the way up to camp and made them crack.

ABBY: They were mine. They were on my bed right before lunch and the next thing I know, during rest hour, Ashley is using them.

ZOE: Thief! Wait, that was to you, Abby. NOT Ashley!

ASHLEY: Thanks for the clarification.

ABBY: And you can't crack them that way by sitting on them.

ZOE: Yes, you can.

ABBY: And why weren't you using them all summer?

ASHLEY: They were in my lockbox.

ABBY: Are you serious?

ASHLEY: I'm very serious. Stealing is a really big crime. Now that that's solved, lets move on.

ABBY: It's not solved.

ASHLEY: Moving on to…drum roll…just kidding…me. Moving on to me.

TRACY: You just went.

ZOE: She was being nice and speaking for Abby. It wasn't her turn.

TRACY: No. Abby, you're allowed to respond now if you want.

ASHLEY: That's not fair. She passed up her turn.

ZOE: Yeah!

ASHLEY: And she did respond. She said sorry.

TRACY: Ash. The rules.

ASHLEY: O K, O K. Abby, you are free to talk...wait for it...NOW!

ABBY: I just want to say. That...that...

ASHLEY: Spit it out.

ABBY: That...that...I don't agree with a lot of what was said tonight.

ASHLEY: What?

TRACY: Don't interrupt!

ABBY: But that I will try to get better or whatever. And also, Zoe, on Saturday you borrowed my camp shirt without asking, ripped out my name tag, cut the neck and stuff to look cooler, and you never gave it back.

ZOE: Didn't do that.

ASHLEY: She didn't.

ZOE: Your shirts are too big.

ASHLEY: Wow, Abby. You should be careful.

TRACY: O K. Moving forward.

ZOE: Now who's left?

ABBY: We have Trac—

ASHLEY: And remember, everyone, no defending yourself.

ZOE: Cough, cough. Abby.

ABBY: I didn't!

ASHLEY: You just have to learn to take the constructive criticism.

TRACY: Cause we all need to get things off of our chest.

ZOE: Off of our tits.

ASHLEY: What??

TRACY: Vagina! Couldn't resist.

SAMANTHA: Can you please be more mature?

ZOE: I don't know what that means.

SAMANTHA: Clearly.

ABBY: O K, so—

ASHLEY: Why are you talking? O K, Tracy, because you're so eager-beaver controlling, no pun intended, you go ahead.

TRACY: That isn't a pun. Anyway, O K, Samantha, I encourage you to participate in more activities. You're always talking about horseback riding but I never see you go. I feel like you are feeling embarrassed cause you're new and think people might make fun of you.

SAMANTHA: Why would anyone make fun of me for horseback riding?

(The girls chuckle.)

TRACY: I don't know. I'm just saying you should be yourself.

SAMANTHA: I am.

TRACY: Like, O K, I'm just going to say it. I know you have the prettiest voice in the bunk. But you never sing for us!

SAMANTHA: Well…

ZOE: Sing for us!

TRACY: I'm so jealous of your voice!

ZOE: Sing!

SAMANTHA: I don't even know what I'd sing.

ABBY: Your Bat Mitzvah invitation!

ASHLEY: Shut up, Abby!

ABBY: What?

TRACY: No, something else. Like Hannah Montana?

ASHLEY: Don't show off for being the only one invited.

ABBY: I'm not.

TRACY: Samantha, sing anything.

ASHLEY: You're just trying to make us all feel excluded, Abigail.

TRACY: I'll even sing with you if you're embarrassed! La la la! I am Samantha!

ASHLEY: Right? Hello?

(No one but ABBY is listening to ASHLEY.)

SAMANTHA: Um…

TRACY: I already sang your Bat Mitzvah invitation so it's your turn. Wait, did I get the tune right?

SAMANTHA: No.

TRACY: Cause that would be AMAZING!

SAMANTHA: You didn't.

TRACY: Just show everyone, Samantha, cause you're really talented.

ASHLEY: How do you know?

TRACY: I heard her in the shower!

SAMANTHA: You heard that? Oh my god! That's so funny! What was I singing?

TRACY: I have no idea! It sounded like something you made up. But it was so good!

SAMANTHA: That's so embarrassing! I can't believe you heard!

TRACY: It's not embarrassing! I didn't want you to stop so I didn't say anything!

ASHLEY: Vomit.

SAMANTHA: So, what should I sing besides Hannah Montana?

TRACY: Sing what you were singing that day…

SAMANTHA: I don't know.

TRACY: Please? You know you're good.

ASHLEY: No one wants to hear you sing.

ABBY: Bragger.

TRACY: I do!

ZOE: Me too!

TRACY: I want to hear if you're actually good.

ZOE: Like better than Ashley.

TRACY: Are you?

SAMANTHA: I don't know.

TRACY/ZOE: Sing!

(SAMANTHA starts to sing a song that she's made up on her own related to Stephanie Meyer's Twilight. *It could be to the tune of* Can You Feel the Love Tonight? *from Disney's* Lion King.)

SAMANTHA: Bella was a simple girl
With a simple plan in life
Until she meets Edward
Will she be his wife?

She does not know why he's different
Until the truth comes out
Edward is a vampire
In this there is no doubt.

Twilight is—

ASHLEY: Ow! My head hurts! Ow!

(ABBY turns the lights back on.)

ABBY: Are you ok?

ZOE: That actually hurt your head?

ASHLEY: Yes. Thank you for that, Samantha. Now I feel sick. So, to get back on topic, I'm just speaking for myself, but we all think it's really rude when you sit out of activities and say that your arm hurts or your back hurts. You were brushing your hair this morning at cleanup at 9:07 to be exact, according to my personal list, and I said, "Isn't that the arm that you can't move?" And then you switched arms. So, that seems pretty weird to me. Just saying.

TRACY: I have the same thing on my list but I crossed it off cause I thought it was mean!

ASHLEY: Great minds think alike.

ZOE: Yeah, why do you get to sit out of soccer and we can't?

TRACY: We are geniuses! Ashley and I will rule the world one day!

SAMANTHA: I don't!

ZOE: Um, you do.

ASHLEY: You can't defend yourself, Samantha. Just take the criticism and try to get better so…

TRACY: So, we don't have to bring it up at the next Bunk Fourteen's Feelings.

ASHLEY: Next!

ABBY: Now whose turn to—

TRACY: Samantha's turn!

(Silence)

ASHLEY: Really? Do you really have nothing to say either? After singing so obnoxiously? (Pause) Alright, I'll speak for—

SAMANTHA: I hooked up with Bryce.

TRACY: What?

ASHLEY: Are you kidding?

ZOE: You can't do that!

ASHLEY: She's lying.

SAMANTHA: No, I'm not.

ABBY: When did you do that?

SAMANTHA: I don't know.

ABBY: See? You don't even know.

ZOE: You don't remember when?

SAMANTHA: Last week or something.

TRACY: What?

ASHLEY: Last week?

SAMANTHA: Yes.

TRACY: Um, I'm hooking up with Bryce.

ZOE: Oh my god, how did you not know that?

ABBY: Yeah. How did you not know that?

SAMANTHA: I did.

ZOE: What? You knew and you still did it! Samantha stuck her tongue down Bryce's throat! And Tracy did too! At the same time! Ew!

TRACY: Not at the same time. Shut up, Zoe.

ABBY: That is so rude.

SAMANTHA: Sorry.

TRACY: Sorry? That's it? What the hell? I was just so nice to you!

ASHLEY: Samantha, you are the slut of the night.

ZOE: Slut of the summer you mean.

ABBY: Summer slut.

ABBY/ZOE: Summer slut! Summer slut!

TRACY: Samantha, how would you feel if I hooked up with your boyfriend?

ASHLEY: Whatever, who cares? Bryce is ugly.

ABBY: No, he's not.

ASHLEY: You like Bryce then?

ZOE: You think he's hot?

ASHLEY: You want to do him?

ZOE: And have his babies?

ASHLEY: Watch out Trace, looks like Abby's in love with your manly man too.

ZOE: It's like a movie!

ASHLEY: What movie?

ZOE: Like, like *Love Actually* or something!

ASHLEY: Ha! Ha! No, it's not! Oh my god, you are so cute and you so need a boyfriend.

TRACY: Whatever, how can you do that to me?

SAMANTHA: I don't know. How can you force everyone to fly to Florida for your Bat Mitzvah and leave me with no one?

TRACY: What? You said you didn't know about us having the same date!

ASHLEY: Ah, the web of lies.

ZOE: Spider web!

ASHLEY: Oh my god, you are so cute. I just want to put you in a little box and carry you around with me everywhere I go!

ABBY: That would be a heavy box.

ZOE: Are you calling me fat?

TRACY: She's not calling you fat, obviously.

ZOE: Am I fat?

ASHLEY: Are you serious? You are the skinniest person in the bunk.

ZOE: Let's vote.

ABBY: No.

ZOE: Yes.

TRACY: No.

ZOE: Yes.

TRACY: Do you guys even care that Samantha hooked up with Bryce? He totally cheated on me!

ASHLEY: Get over it.

ZOE: Yeah, get over it. At least no one called you fat.

ASHLEY: Who thinks Zoe is the skinniest person in the bunk?

ZOE: Um, why aren't you raising your hands? Oh my god! You guys think I'm fat!

ABBY/SAMANTHA/ZOE: We're not voting!

ASHLEY: Fine. It just means that you are the skinniest person and everyone's jealous.

ZOE: Are you still going to put me in a box and stuff?

ASHLEY: Oh my god, Zoe, I was joking! You are so fucking cute!

TRACY: I'm still mad.

ASHLEY: We'll mess with Bryce later. Don't worry.

TRACY: When?

ASHLEY: Tonight.

TRACY: What are you talking about?

ASHLEY: Well, it's my turn to confess something: We are going on a raid!

ABBY: I'm not going.

ASHLEY: Yes, you are.

ABBY: You can't make me.

ASHLEY: Um, yes I can.

TRACY: Well, good. What are we doing to Bryce?

ASHLEY: Revenge. I like it.

TRACY: I'm pissed off. He dry humped me yesterday and I let him do it even though his dick was hitting the side of my vagina really hard over and over.

ZOE: Ew! Hahaha!

ASHLEY: That asshole.

ABBY: Samantha, did Bryce dry hump you?

SAMANTHA: Yeah.

TRACY: Seriously?

SAMANTHA: And he touched both my boobs.

ZOE: What?

ASHLEY: With his tongue?

SAMANTHA: Ew, no.

ASHLEY: Why is that "ew"?

SAMANTHA: Because it is.

ZOE: Does your boob taste weird or something?

SAMANTHA: I don't know Zoe, why don't you try licking it?

TRACY: I don't think you hooked up with him.

ZOE: You want me to lick your boob?

TRACY: I think you're just saying you did.

ZOE: Cause that would make you a lesbian.

ABBY: Oh my god, yes!

TRACY: Cause you're still mad about the whole Bat Mitzvah thing. Right, Sam?

ASHLEY: Call her *Samantha*.

TRACY: Were you making it up?

ABBY: You lied about it?

SAMANTHA: No.

ABBY: Yes you did.

ASHLEY: She's lying.

ZOE: And she's a lesbian.

SAMANTHA: Stop saying that!

ZOE: I'm not requesting you next summer if you're a lesbian.

ASHLEY: Understandable.

ZOE: I mean, I won't feel safe if you're watching me get undressed and stuff.

ABBY: No more pickling with Samantha.

SAMANTHA: I don't like to— Can't you just call it spooning?

ABBY: We're too tempting for you to share a bed with?

ZOE: Cause I'm so hot and sexy?

ABBY: I know someone who thinks Ashley's hot and sexy!

ZOE: Who?

ASHLEY: Abby, do you want to die?

TRACY: Samantha, I complimented you so much on your voice.

ABBY: I didn't mean—

SAMANTHA: You can't be nice to me like once and expect me to not hook up with people who like me.

ASHLEY: Ahhhh! Pause for a second. I have something to say.

TRACY: No, we're not done—

ASHLEY: Tracy, you would be the prettiest in the bunk if you didn't have a uni-brow.

TRACY: My mom is taking me at the end of the summer to get it waxed.

(ZOE feels TRACY's uni-brow.)

TRACY: Don't touch it!

ZOE: It's fuzzy.

ASHLEY: No one would cheat on you if you had two eyebrows. That's all I'm saying.

ZOE: Tweeze them!

TRACY: No! I'm getting them waxed, I said. You're not supposed to tweeze if you're getting them waxed.

ASHLEY: Who says?

ABBY: I heard that too.

ZOE: It will be so fun! Please?

ASHLEY: Please? Please, can I tweeze them? I promise I'm so good at it.

ABBY: She is good at it.

ASHLEY: See?

TRACY: I don't know.

SAMANTHA: Oh my god, just do it.

ASHLEY: Even Samantha thinks you should.

ZOE: And she's like a lesbian so you'll be hotter if you tweeze!

ASHLEY: That makes zero sense.

ABBY: You are so funny!

ASHLEY: No one was talking to you.

ZOE: Come on, please, Tracy?

ASHLEY: Please?

ABBY: I have really good tweezers.

ASHLEY: We're using mine. Please?

ZOE: Please?

ASHLEY: I'll be your best friend.

TRACY: Fine.

ASHLEY/ZOE: Yay!

TRACY: Be careful though and don't touch the part above the eyebrow.

ASHLEY: But that's the worst part.

TRACY: Don't do that part or I'm not letting you do anything.

ABBY: Fine.

ASHLEY: Why are you saying fine? You're not tweezing.

ABBY: I'm helping though.

SAMANTHA: I'm writing. Let me know when you want to resume the meeting.

(They tweeze her eyebrows. ZOE videotapes with her camera. TRACY screams, "Vagina" throughout the procedure. ASHLEY finishes.)

ASHLEY: Wait, don't look yet.

TRACY: Oh my god, oh my god.

ASHLEY: O K, open!

(TRACY looks in the mirror.)

TRACY: I look so hot.

SAMANTHA: Conceited.

ASHLEY: Shut up, she does look hot.

ZOE: Way hotter than you.

ABBY: You are so pretty.

ZOE: Yeah, you look like so good.

ASHLEY: I'd let you give me a blowjob if I were a man.

TRACY: Oh, vagina, vagina, vagina.

(ABBY *takes a picture of* TRACY'*s newly plucked
face.* ASHLEY *happens to be in the picture as well and
consequently screams.*)

ABBY: What the fuck?

ASHLEY: Exactly. What the fuck.

ABBY: What?

ASHLEY: You took a picture.

ABBY: So?

ASHLEY: Of me.

ABBY: It was of Tracy.

ASHLEY: I'm in it.

ABBY: Oh.

ZOE: Oh my god! I have an idea!

ASHLEY: What do you mean, "Oh"?

ABBY: I'll delete it.

ZOE: I'm starting a fashion contest!

ABBY/TRACY: Yeah!

ZOE: Then I'll prove to everyone how skinny I am!

TRACY: I happen to love my body. My mom says it's
ADORABLE.

ZOE: Yeah, but I'm the skinniest.

ABBY: I have the best hips.

ASHLEY: That's cause you're fat.

TRACY: Wait, O K, everyone go get your best outfit for...um...

ZOE: Camp prom!

ABBY/TRACY: Yeah!

TRACY: O K, we have five seconds. Get your dresses on and enter from the bathroom.

ASHLEY: I'm the judge!

(ABBY, TRACY, *and* ZOE *grab dresses and exit to the bathroom.*)

TRACY: Samantha, are you doing it?

SAMANTHA: Um, I—

ABBY: Does it look like we invited you?

ASHLEY: Woah.

TRACY: Just go if you want to go.

ASHLEY: Abby, put some music on!

TRACY: O K, one at a time, enter. Wait for it, wait for it. Now!

(ABBY *plays the song* I Got It From My Mama *by will.i.am.* TRACY *struts into the bunk with pizzazz and attitude. She improvises a lap dance on* ASHLEY *who is judging with her moshi pillow on her head.* ABBY *and* ZOE *peek out from the bathroom.* SAMANTHA *is watching, but certainly not participating in the fun. This is stupid to her.*)

ASHLEY: Ten!

TRACY: Vagina, I'm awesome. My vagina, is awesome!

ASHLEY: Oh my god, Tracy, you are on crack.

TRACY: You know it!

ASHLEY: Next!

ZOE: Where did I get this body from? I got it from my mama!

(ZOE *struts out awkwardly, trying to be sexy.* ABBY, ASHLEY, *and* TRACY *are hysterically laughing. She attempts to do a bend and snap, referencing* Legally Blonde, *but fails miserably. All the more funny)*

ASHLEY: Eleven!

TRACY: It's out of ten!

ASHLEY: Fifteen!

ZOE: Yay!

ASHLEY: I'm dying! I'm dying! You are so funny!

ZOE: Was I the sexiest mama?

ASHLEY: Ha! Ha! Stop! You are so cute!

ZOE: You are so cute.

ABBY: That's so cute.

ASHLEY: What's cute?

ZOE: Yeah, what's cute?

ABBY: Um. I don't know. You girls are cute?

(Pause.)

ASHLEY: Thanks!

ZOE: Yeah, thanks.

TRACY: Next to next to the N-E-X-T next!

ABBY: Are you ready?

ASHLEY/TRACY/ZOE: Yes!

(ABBY skips out enthusiastically.)

ASHLEY: Go home!

ZOE: Ew.

TRACY: Whooooo!

ASHLEY: You're disgusting!

ZOE: Yucky!

TRACY: Go, Abby!

ASHLEY: You're fat!

(ABBY *pulls at her dress self-consciously; it's rather pathetic.* ABBY *poses enthusiastically, attempting to triumph over* ASHLEY *and* ZOE's *comments, but upon seeing no positive reaction, winces and sits down in pain.*)

ASHLEY: Oh my god, can you please stop faking your injuries?

(SAMANTHA *turns off the music.*)

ABBY: Wait, do I really look fat? *(Silence)* Do I? Do I?

ASHLEY: Shot not saying the truth again.

TRACY/ZOE: Shot not!

SAMANTHA: I'll say something.

ABBY: I don't care what you have to say.

SAMANTHA: I'm just trying to help.

ASHLEY: Cause you're so helpful.

SAMANTHA: I have fiber gummy bears.

ASHLEY: You have those?

SAMANTHA: Yeah.

ASHLEY: How?

TRACY: They make you poop out all your fat! Gross!

SAMANTHA: I got them from my mama.

ASHLEY: She just gave them to you?

SAMANTHA: Yes. Is that a problem?

ASHLEY: I've been talking about how much I want them like this whole summer and you didn't say a single word about it.

SAMANTHA: Maybe I didn't want to share them with you.

ZOE: Rudeness.

TRACY: That's B-I-T-C—

SAMANTHA: Bitchy, Tracy. I know how to spell. So, do you want them?

ASHLEY: Well, they obviously don't work for you, so no thanks.

SAMANTHA: I was talking to Abby.

ABBY: Yeah, well, Ashley's right. You're not skinny so they obviously don't work.

SAMANTHA: Your loss.

ASHLEY: I'll help you, Abby.

ABBY: How?

ASHLEY: I'll show you what I do when I feel fat.

ABBY: You're not fat!

ASHLEY: I never said I was.

ABBY: Oh.

ASHLEY: Get that empty Tostitos bag.

ABBY: O K.

ASHLEY: O K, Zoe, come here.

ZOE: What?

ASHLEY: Hold open the bag in front of Abby's face.

ZOE: O K.

TRACY: What are you doing?

ASHLEY: Take your two fingers and shove them down your throat.

ABBY: Ew, no!

TRACY: Ha! That is so disgusting!

ASHLEY: Do it.

ABBY: I'm scared.

SAMANTHA: It's not that bad.

ASHLEY: Do it.

ZOE: Do it!

TRACY: That's sicktastic. I would never do that.

ASHLEY: Do it!

ABBY: I'm trying.

ASHLEY: Deeper.

ABBY: Ew, ew, ew.

ASHLEY: Stop talking or else it doesn't work. Shove them down your throat.

ABBY: I'll gag if I do that.

ASHLEY: Exactly. Do it.

TRACY: Abby, don't do it. You're freaking me out.

ZOE: I want her to throw up!

TRACY: You're all insane.

ABBY: I can't.

TRACY: Thank you!

ASHLEY: Boring.

(ASHLEY *grabs* ZOE*'s camera and takes a picture of* ZOE *holding the empty Tostitos bag and* ABBY *with two fingers down her throat.*)

ABBY: What was that for?

ASHLEY: Inspiration. For next time you want to try it.

TRACY: Never try it again, puh-lease!

ASHLEY: Let's do a séance!

(ABBY, TRACY, *and* ZOE *start changing out of their dresses. They know exactly how to take off their dresses and put their pajamas back on without exposing themselves at all.*

You learn these things at camp. Or they might just throw a sweatshirt on and worry about the dress later.)

ZOE: Oh my god! Remember, yesterday, when we were talking about Christy's yeast infection?

ABBY: That's so funny.

ASHLEY: Why is that funny?

ABBY: Oh. I don't know.

ASHLEY: What's funny is that Zoe thought yeast infections only grow on pizza!

(ABBY, ASHLEY, TRACY, *and* ZOE *laugh hysterically.)*

ZOE: I don't get it! I still don't get it!

ABBY: In a few years you will.

ASHLEY: You probably don't get it either, Abby.

ZOE: Oh, I have a confession first.

TRACY: No, you can't. We all went already—

ZOE: I farted while pickling with Tracy last night and no one knew who it was!

TRACY: Ew. You are never pickling with me again.

ZOE: Haha! Oops!

TRACY: Well, fine, then I have a confession. Last night, I sharted in your face.

SAMANTHA: That's disgusting.

TRACY: I shart, I fart, I have a real big heart. I hump, I dump, I hate those that jump. Jump and cheat that is. That is my intro rap to let you know, Samantha, not that I want to bring it up again, but that if you actually hooked up with Bryce, I'm waiting for a real sorry.

ABBY: She just wants you to be honest.

TRACY: And it is the opposite of honest what you're doing.

SAMANTHA: O K, I'll be honest.

TRACY: What does that mean?

SAMANTHA: It means I'll be honest.

TRACY: Good, cause you should be hon—

SAMANTHA: So, I'm just going to throw it out there that I HONESTLY know for a fact that someone in this bunk got their period yesterday and didn't tell anyone.

ZOE: What?

ASHLEY: Are you serious?

ABBY: Who?

SAMANTHA: I can't say.

ASHLEY: Say it.

ABBY: Wait, whoever got their period, can you just tell us? We'd all tell you.

ASHLEY: Honesty, people, honesty.

ZOE: Who is it?

ASHLEY: Samantha, tell us.

SAMANTHA: Nope.

ASHLEY: Tell us or we'll tell Bryce you're a whore.

ABBY: He already knows that!

ASHLEY: Don't be a bitch.

SAMANTHA: Have fun figuring it out.

ZOE: Well, it wasn't me!

ASHLEY: Duh. And I already have mine.

ABBY: Wasn't me!

TRACY: Wasn't me!

ASHLEY: It was Tracy!

TRACY: No, it wasn't.

ZOE: Yes, it was.

TRACY: I swear it wasn't me!

ASHLEY: Then why did you deny it and say it wasn't you?

TRACY: Because it wasn't!

ABBY: Then why did you say it last?

TRACY: I don't know!

SAMANTHA: Well, Tracy HONESTLY told me yesterday she's not supposed to get it for another year. So, I mean, it can't be her.

ASHLEY: How do you know that?

TRACY: Doctors know that type of stuff.

ZOE: Really? I want to know when I'm getting it.

ASHLEY: I still think it's Tracy.

TRACY: Well, it's not me.

ASHLEY: Prove it.

TRACY: What? No way.

ASHLEY: Yeah. Show me your underwear.

TRACY: That I'm wearing?

ASHLEY: Yeah.

ZOE: Gross.

ASHLEY: No. Fine. Show me your underwear from yesterday.

TRACY: I'm not doing that.

ZOE: Oh, yeah! She sharted in that!

ASHLEY: Oh my god.

ZOE: What?

ASHLEY: Oh my god!

ABBY: What?

ASHLEY: Zoe, you totally slept in Tracy's bed last night! You pickled with Tracy while she had her period!

(ABBY *and* ZOE *scream.*)

TRACY: Stop it! Just stop!

ZOE: That's the grossest thing I've ever heard!

ASHLEY: Find her dirty underwear, Abby.

ABBY: Ew!

ASHLEY: Do it!

ABBY: Fine.

(ABBY *looks for the underwear, her head fully immersed in* TRACY's *laundry bag.*)

TRACY: Stop doing that. Seriously.

ASHLEY: Someone's P M S-ing.

ZOE: Haha!

TRACY: Seriously, I said!

SAMANTHA: Do you even know what that means?

TRACY: Abby, stop!

ZOE: What?

SAMANTHA: P M S.

ZOE: Yeah.

TRACY: Abby!

SAMANTHA: What does it mean then?

ZOE: People… Making… Surprise?

ASHLEY: Oh my god. I'm peeing in my pants. Oh my god. Zoe, you are so cute!

ABBY: Found it!

ASHLEY: Show us!

ZOE: Gross! It's all brown and red!

SAMANTHA: I'm going to throw up.

ZOE: I'm the one who pickled with her last night!

TRACY: O K, so what? I got my period. Big fucking deal.

ASHLEY: Get out your camera!

ZOE: Me?

ASHLEY: Yeah!

ZOE: O K, hold on.

TRACY: Stop! Don't, Zoe.

ZOE: I'm putting it on Pets & Kids setting.

TRACY: Stop!

ASHLEY: Pets & Kids!

ZOE: Cause Tracy is a kid—

ASHLEY: No, she's a woman now!

ZOE: O K, so Tracy used to be a kid—

ASHLEY: And her pet is—

ZOE: Her period blood!

ASHLEY: Oh my god! Oh my god! You are so cute!

ZOE: You are cute!

SAMANTHA: I might throw up. Honestly.

ASHLEY: Oh my god, you should videotape it too.

ZOE: O K.

ASHLEY: Zoom in on the blood. Abby, hold it out so Zoe can see it.

ABBY: This is the most disgusting thing ever.

ASHLEY: Your dad's a doctor so you should be used to this.

ZOE: Yeah, you probably do this all the time.

ABBY: Do what?

ZOE: Like, play with period blood.

ABBY: No, I don't.

ZOE: Samantha's mom probably does it for your dad at work cause she's his secretary.

ABBY: Shut up.

ASHLEY: No, they just fuck.

SAMANTHA: Shut up.

ZOE: Her name is on it.

ASHLEY: Zoom in on her name. It's on mute, right?

(ZOE *makes a disgusting face in the camera, zooms in on* TRACY, *who is mortified, and then focuses again on* TRACY's *stained underwear.*)

TRACY: You better delete that.

ASHLEY: It's part of our documentary.

ZOE: So…

ASHLEY: So…

ASHLEY/ZOE: Nope!

ASHLEY: Sorry.

ZOE: Yeah, sorry.

TRACY: Don't apologize if you don't mean it.

ASHLEY: I do mean it!

ZOE: I do mean it!

SAMANTHA: You're copying her again.

ASHLEY: Shut up, Samantha.

ZOE: Are you using a tampon?

TRACY: No.

ASHLEY: Why not?

TRACY: I'm using a pad.

ASHLEY: Gross. So much cleaner if you use a tampon.

TRACY: Whatever, when I'm ready to use one I will.

ZOE: What if you get it on your Bat Mitzvah?

TRACY: I don't know.

ASHLEY: That's why we have to teach you how to use a tampon. Abby, thank you for your help.

ABBY: No problem.

ASHLEY: Now, would you be so kind as to get me one of my tampons?

ABBY: Uh, yeah. Wait, what do I do with the underwear?

ASHLEY: You're still holding it??

ABBY: Well, yeah.

ASHLEY: Ew, Abby.

ZOE: You're gross.

TRACY: Just put it back in the laundry.

ASHLEY: Boring answer.

ABBY: Well, can you please tell me what to do cause it's bloody and nasty to hold.

ASHLEY: True.

ABBY: Here!

(ABBY *flings the underwear at* SAMANTHA. *It lands on her journal while she's writing in it.*)

SAMANTHA: Oh my god!

(ABBY, ASHLEY, *and* ZOE *laugh hysterically.*)

SAMANTHA: Ew, get it off! Get it off!

TRACY: Seriously? Stop!

ASHLEY: Abby, get it.

ABBY: Throw it back.

SAMANTHA: You think I'm touching this?

TRACY: Give it to me!

(SAMANTHA *flings the stained underwear off of her journal without touching it.*)

ZOE: Hang it on the flagpole!

ASHLEY: Yes!

TRACY: No!

ASHLEY: That would be the funniest thing ever.

ZOE: Ew, the blood's like gonna drip on the flagpole.

TRACY: Don't be obnoxious. Give it back to me. Oh my god!

ASHLEY: O K, yeah that would be mean. Sorry, Tracy.

ABBY: But so funny!

ASHLEY: Don't be a bitch, Abby. It has her name on it.

TRACY: Put it in my laundry. Please.

ASHLEY: So, I won't hang it on the flagpole if…

TRACY: What?

ASHLEY: If…you let me teach you how to put a tampon in.

TRACY: Um…

ABBY: Just say yes so I can put this down.

TRACY: Fine.

ZOE: I want my period.

TRACY: No, you don't.

ZOE: Yeah, I want to bleed out of my vagina.

ASHLEY: Zoe, one day you will.

ABBY: Me too!

ASHLEY: One day, we will all have blood pour from our cunts.

TRACY: Bad word! Bad word! Cunt.

ASHLEY: Tracy, come into the bathroom.

ZOE: I'm coming!

ABBY: Me too!

ASHLEY: No, this is very private. Just me, Tracy, her vagina...and Zoe.

ZOE: Yes!

ABBY: But Tracy wants me there, right?

(ASHLEY, TRACY, *and* ZOE *exit to the bathroom.* ABBY *follows, and* ASHLEY *slams the door in* ABBY's *face.*)

SAMANTHA: I'd vomit.

(ABBY *and* SAMANTHA *are left alone on stage. After a few lines,* SAMANTHA *puts her headphones in, and* ABBY *is left listening all by herself by the door.*)

ASHLEY: Open it.

TRACY: I can't.

ASHLEY: That's just the plastic. Whatever, I'll do it.

TRACY: O K.

ASHLEY: Stick this part in the hole.

ABBY: (*At the door*) Oh my god.

TRACY: Aren't there two holes?

ASHLEY: I don't know. I think.

ABBY: (*Through the door*) There are!

TRACY: (*To* ABBY) What?

ASHLEY: Just shove it in.

ZOE: I want to shove it in!

ASHLEY: When you have blood coming out of you, I'll let you shove one up your own vagina.

TRACY: O K.

ASHLEY: Is it up really deep?

TRACY: Yeah, it hurts.

ASHLEY: That's cause you're a virgin.

ABBY: *(To* SAMANTHA*)* Ashley would know.

*(*SAMANTHA *stares at* ABBY *without any expression of acknowledgment or understanding and looks back down.)*

TRACY: Ow.

ASHLEY: Now, push the bottom thing up. Like you're injecting a shot.

TRACY: No, I'm scared.

ABBY: You can do it, Tracy!

ASHLEY: Shut up, Abby. Go away.

TRACY: I can't.

ASHLEY: Just do it.

TRACY: Vagina, vagina, vagina.

ZOE: I'll do it.

TRACY: No.

ZOE: I can do it! I see it. I'll just push it up for you.

ASHLEY: Fine. Let her do it.

TRACY: Are you watching her?

ASHLEY: Yeah. Don't worry.

ABBY: *(To* SAMANTHA*)* She's letting Zoe do it.

*(*SAMANTHA *looks up, doesn't respond, looks down.)*

ZOE: Oh my god. Oh my god. Oh my god.

TRACY: Ow.

ASHLEY: I think she did it.

ABBY: *(Whispers to* SAMANTHA*)* She did it, I think.

*(*SAMANTHA *doesn't hear. She doesn't even look up.* ABBY *turns back to the door.)*

TRACY: Is it in?

ASHLEY: Yup, there's the string.

ZOE: Yay!

TRACY: O K, am I done?

ASHLEY: You're welcome.

ZOE: You're welcome.

TRACY: Thanks.

*(*ASHLEY, TRACY, *and* ZOE *enter and push* ABBY *out of the way.)*

ASHLEY: You are totally going to raise the flag for this tomorrow.

TRACY: I don't want to.

ASHLEY: She did it!

ZOE: She did it but I pushed it in!

ASHLEY: Yeah, I have that part on video.

TRACY: What?

ASHLEY: I taped Zoe shoving it up your hole.

TRACY: Are you serious?

ASHLEY: Um, yeah.

TRACY: Wait, let me see.

ASHLEY: No.

TRACY: Why not?

ASHLEY: It's Zoe's camera.

TRACY: Zoe, can I see it?

ZOE: No.

TRACY: It's my vagina.

ASHLEY: Sorry.

ZOE: Yeah, sorry.

ASHLEY: It's for the documentary.

ABBY: What documentary?

TRACY: You can't put that online.

ASHLEY: Why not?

ZOE: People would like see that and be like, "Ew, that's Tracy's vagina!"

ABBY: How would they know it's hers?

ASHLEY: I don't know. How many people have you hooked up with, Tracy?

ABBY: Bryce is one.

TRACY: He hasn't seen my vagina if that's what you're thinking.

ASHLEY: I don't know. Is that what I'm thinking?

SAMANTHA: Disgusting.

ZOE: He'll find it and totally know!

TRACY: No, he won't.

ASHLEY: He'll jerk off to it every night.

SAMANTHA: More like it'll make him throw up.

ASHLEY: And then his dad will jerk off to it too.

SAMANTHA: Vomit.

ABBY: Ashley's not lying! She knows—

ASHLEY: I can destroy you. Tracy, is that why Bryce dry humped you?

TRACY: What do you mean?

ASHLEY: Like, he would have fingered you and seen your vagina, but you have your period so you didn't want blood on his finger?

TRACY: Maybe.

ASHLEY: I'm so good!

ZOE: Wow!

ABBY: How did you think of that?

ASHLEY: I'm not retarded.

ABBY: Did it hurt?

ASHLEY: What?

ABBY: Not you. Tracy, did it hurt?

TRACY: The tampon?

ABBY: Yeah.

TRACY: Just like a little bit.

ASHLEY: See, what would you do without your best friends?

ABBY: When did you use tampons?

ASHLEY: Immediately.

ABBY: Who taught you?

ASHLEY: I'm not stupid. I taught myself.

ABBY: Did Ryan finger you this summer?

TRACY: Duh, he fingered her.

ZOE: You didn't know that?

ABBY: Did you have your period?

ASHLEY: Not when he fingered me.

ABBY: Did it, like—

ASHLEY: Like what?

ABBY: Hurt?

ASHLEY: Um, no. When guys finger you, it doesn't hurt.

ABBY: How many times did Ryan finger you?

ASHLEY: I don't know.

ABBY: Like a lot?

ASHLEY: Yes, Abby, like a lot.

TRACY: What does it feel like?

ASHLEY: Like a finger is up your vagina.

ZOE: Ow!

ABBY: Are you going to return the favor?

ASHLEY: That's none of your business.

ZOE: What favor?

ASHLEY: You'll understand in a few years.

ZOE: You always say that. I don't get it! I don't get it!

ABBY: I meant—

ASHLEY: Shut up.

ABBY: Sorry.

ASHLEY: She meant sex.

ABBY: No, I didn't.

ASHLEY: Well, then what did you possibly mean?

ABBY: I meant like jerking off or something.

ASHLEY: What?

ABBY: I don't know.

ASHLEY: Exactly. You don't know.

ABBY: Fine, sex. Returning the favor. Sex.

ASHLEY: If you think jerking a guy off is going to satisfy him, you're wrong.

ABBY: It's just that isn't sex a big step after just fingering or whatever?

ASHLEY: Why, Abby, do you think I'm a slut?

ABBY: What?

ASHLEY: Do you?

ABBY: I never said that.

ASHLEY: But you thought it, didn't you?

ABBY: No, cause you're not a slut if it's like...

ASHLEY: Like what?

ABBY: Like...

ASHLEY: Like what?

ABBY: Forced or something. I don't know.

ASHLEY: You don't know. You don't know ANYTHING. You've never even hooked up.

ABBY: Yes, I have.

ASHLEY: Don't be a bitch, Abby, O K?

ABBY: I'm sorry.

ASHLEY: Cause I'll kill you.

TRACY: What the hell?

ABBY: I won't say anything. Pinky swear.

ASHLEY: And you haven't hooked up, so don't pretend you have experience when you don't even have any pubic hair yet. You're such a baby.

ABBY: So, what? Everyone develops at different rates.

ASHLEY: Even Zoe has hair down there and she is like the cutest thing in the world.

ZOE: Yeah, I have eight hairs there.

TRACY: Vagina.

ASHLEY: Oh my god, you are so cute. O K, let's just do a séance or something!

ABBY: You. I hooked up with you.

ZOE: Me?

ABBY: No, you. Ashley, you.

ASHLEY: Oh my god, Abby. You are so immature. That wasn't hooking up!

ZOE: Yeah, that wasn't. What are you talking about?

ABBY: You weren't even there, Zoe.

ASHLEY: I was showing you how cause you wanted it so badly. You like want to be raped or something.

TRACY/ZOE: *(Chant in unison)* R-A-P-E
Get your penis out of me!

ABBY: Yeah, but we kissed with tongue and that counts.

ASHLEY: No, it doesn't. Oh, and then you licked my retainer, you freak. What are you, a lesbian too or something?

ZOE: Oh my god. Are you?

ABBY: No!

ASHLEY: Good. Cause if you were that would be so weird!

ZOE: We'd have two lesbians in the bunk. Lesbian sisters.

ABBY: Over my dead body we'll be sisters.

SAMANTHA: Shut up, Abby.

ZOE: You could be lesbians together and make lesbian children!

ASHLEY: Zoe, you're so cute! A lesbian can't get a girl preggers!

ZOE: Why not?

ABBY: Because you need the—

ASHLEY: Shut up, Abby. Because, Zoe, it's just not possible. I'll explain why to you later.

ZOE: O K. I don't get it.

ASHLEY: You don't get a lot of things.

ZOE: Like what?

ASHLEY: Like anything. Like masturbation, orgasms, popping cherries, blow-jobs. ANYTHING.

SAMANTHA: Shh. Can we not?

ZOE: No, we have to talk about stuff or else we'll never learn.

TRACY: Well, if we go to mess with Bryce later, then you can learn first hand, Zoe.

ZOE: Oh my god. Tonight? I'm hooking up tonight?

TRACY: Who should she hook up with?

ZOE: Um, Jake.

TRACY: Yes! You should!

ABBY: If he wants to.

ZOE: Are you saying he's not gonna want to hook up with me? I'm so sexy.

ASHLEY: Can I just like shrink you and put you in my pocket? You are so cute.

ZOE: Not cute! Sexy!

ASHLEY: But we all have to stay up. Samantha, stop falling asleep!

SAMANTHA: I'm not. *(She puts her headphones in.)*

ASHLEY: Yes, you are.

ZOE: How do I do it? Like hook up.

ASHLEY: Let the guy lead.

TRACY: Don't write your name with your tongue.

ASHLEY: Tonguing your name as a correct method is a myth. It obliterates relationships.

ZOE: What?

TRACY: And you have to figure out what you're going to talk about before and after.

ASHLEY: Yeah, like something casual so it's not awkward.

TRACY: But you have to transition into the kiss.

ZOE: Oh my god, I'm so scared.

ASHLEY: Like, slow down conversation and bite your lip to bring attention to it.

TRACY: Whore!

ASHLEY: What? It works.

ZOE: Like this?

ASHLEY: Try making out with your hand.

ZOE: Like this?

ASHLEY: Um, sort of.

TRACY: Slower.

ASHLEY: And now touch yourself.

ZOE: Like this?

ASHLEY: Your vagina, Zoe.

TRACY: Vagina!

ZOE: Why?

ASHLEY: It turns them on.

ZOE: Oh.

TRACY: Zoe, you don't have to do that.

ASHLEY: It's hot.

ZOE: I don't get it.

TRACY: Just concentrate on the kiss.

ASHLEY: Fine, don't listen to me.

ZOE: What? I'm listening.

ASHLEY: Spin the bottle.

ZOE: What?

ASHLEY: We're going to play a round of spin the bottle so you can practice on real people.

ZOE: But there are lesbians in the bunk.

ASHLEY: Zoe, do you want to hook up tonight or not?

ZOE: I do!

ASHLEY: Then let's do it.

TRACY: I have my Paul Mitchell mousse bottle we could use.

ASHLEY: Good, get it. O K, everyone circle up. Samantha, stop falling asleep!

SAMANTHA: What?

ABBY: Whatever, she never plays anything. She might as well not exist.

(ABBY, ASHLEY, TRACY, and ZOE all circle up.)

ASHLEY: O K, Zoe, spin.

ZOE: I'm scared.

TRACY: Get me.

ZOE: I'll try. One, two, three…I'm scared.

ASHLEY/TRACY: Do it!

ZOE: I don't want to practice on Abby!

ASHLEY: Abby, move out of the circle.

ABBY: No, I'm playing!

ASHLEY: Gross. Just don't let it land on her. Ready, go!

(ZOE spins the bottle, and it lands on ABBY.)

ZOE: Ew. No!

ASHLEY: Do it.

TRACY: Oh my god, this is H-I-L-arious!

ABBY: What do I do?

ASHLEY: Blind leading the blind.

TRACY: Meet in the middle. O K. Now, Abby, put your arms around Zoe's waist.

ASHLEY: Less like she has a disease.

ZOE: I don't have any diseases, I promise.

ASHLEY: Zoe, put your arms around Abby's neck.

TRACY: Like you're dancing at a Bat Mitzvah!

ASHLEY: Look into each other's eyes.

TRACY: Oh my god. Oh my god.

ZOE: Stop staring at me!

ABBY: Ashley said to look into each other's eyes.

ZOE: O K, fine, now what?

TRACY: Both lean in.

ABBY/ZOE: Ow!

ASHLEY: Oh my god, Abby!

ZOE: My head!

TRACY: Go for the lips.

ABBY: Stop moving away.

ZOE: Your breath smells like cough medicine. It's gross.

ABBY: I have a cough. I can't help it.

ZOE: Then why am I hooking up with you?

ASHLEY: Forget it.

(ASHLEY *violently rips* ABBY *off of* ZOE *and then kisses* ZOE *aggressively.*)

ABBY: And you called me a lesbian.

ASHLEY: You are such a cunt.

TRACY: Bad word! Bad word! Cunt.

ABBY: It's not bad or anything. I just wasn't raised that way.

ASHLEY: What way?

ZOE: Your sister lover Samantha was raised that way.

ASHLEY: I said, what way?

ABBY: Samantha is not my sister or my lover or my friend!

TRACY: Is she sleeping?

ZOE: Did you just sleep through my first sexy hook up?

TRACY: That wasn't sexy.

ZOE: You're probably not sexy when you hook up either!

TRACY: No. I am.

ASHLEY: She is.

ASHLEY: *Samantha!*

TRACY: Samantha!

ZOE: Sammi!

ABBY: Sam!

(SAMANTHA *has fallen asleep with her headphones in.*)

ASHLEY: O K, well, there's only one thing to do.

ZOE: What?

ABBY: *(Overlapping with* ASHLEY*)* Shaving cream!

ASHLEY: *(Overlapping with* ABBY*)* Séance!

TRACY: Oh my god, yes! Put it on her hands and tickle her face!

ASHLEY: Séance!

ZOE: Yes, tickle-tickle!

ABBY: You are so cute!

ASHLEY: We're doing a séance, I said.

TRACY: My mom packed me with seven bottles of shaving cream for some reason.

ZOE: She's weird.

TRACY: I know!

ABBY/TRACY/ZOE: Sh–sh–sh–sh–shaving cream! Sh–sh–sh–sh–shaving cream!

TRACY: Get all her clothes.

ABBY: How did she fall asleep already? What a loser.

TRACY: Zoe, get all her bras out.

ZOE: O K.

TRACY: And I'll do her socks!

ZOE: What are you going to do with her socks?

TRACY: Fill them with shaving cream. Duh.

ABBY: That's so funny!

TRACY: Someone get her shirts and stuff. Abby?

ABBY: O K!

TRACY: Woah, sexy.

ABBY: Oh my god!

ZOE: That one's leopard!

TRACY: Wait, does shaving cream stain?

ASHLEY: No.

TRACY: Are you sure?

ASHLEY: I'm not stupid.

(ABBY *and* ZOE *go crazy with the shaving cream.* TRACY *is more conservative with her usage.* ABBY *sprays shaving cream in the shape of a penis on Samantha's Jonas Brothers poster.* ASHLEY *videotapes with* ZOE'S *camera.*)

ABBY: Did you see what I did? It's a penis!

ASHLEY: Congratulations.

ABBY: Look, Zoe, a penis!

ZOE: Penis!

ASHLEY: Abby, go to the poster.

ABBY: O K. Why?

ASHLEY: You're so funny! Put your hand at the top and grip it like you're really proud.

ABBY: I'm proud! I'm proud!

(ASHLEY *motions to* ZOE *to go over to* ABBY. ZOE *jumps on* ABBY's *arm, which tears the poster down.* ASHLEY *laughs.*)

ABBY: Ow, you hurt my arm.

ASHLEY: Go cry about it.

TRACY: That can't be good.

ABBY: Wait, did anyone get her underwear?

ASHLEY: You do it.

ABBY: Where is it?

TRACY: Vagina!

ZOE: It's here.

(ZOE *pulls out a bracelet from one of* SAMANTHA's *drawers.*)

ZOE: Look, Abby! Samantha has the same bracelet as you! Now you're more like twins.

ABBY: Ew, I hate that bracelet.

TRACY: I thought you liked it cause your dad got it for you.

ABBY: I hate it now. (*She tears off her green bracelet and sprays it with shaving cream.*) Give me another bottle. I ran out.

TRACY: Already?

ZOE: Here. I don't shave yet.

ASHLEY: Oh my god, Zoe, you have to learn how to shave! I'll do it for you later.

TRACY: You should do it before you hook up tonight.

ZOE: Shave? Tonight?

ASHLEY: No one'll hook up with you if you have hairy legs.

ZOE: But they're light.

TRACY: True, but—

ASHLEY: So not an excuse.

ABBY: Oh, wow!

ZOE: What?

ABBY: You guys are gonna love me in like two seconds!

ASHLEY: Doubt it.

TRACY/ZOE: What?

ABBY: I found her invitation!

TRACY: The C D?

ABBY: Yeah!

ASHLEY: No one cares.

TRACY: Oh my god, give it to me!

ABBY: Here!

ASHLEY: No, give it to me.

(ABBY *has already handed the C D off to* TRACY. ASHLEY *is ignored.*)

TRACY: This is going to be UNBELIEVABLE!

ZOE: She sings on it?

ABBY: Yeah!

TRACY: She probably sounds AMAZING.

ZOE: Play it!

TRACY: I only have iPod speakers. Who has a C D player?

ZOE: Not me!

TRACY: Does anyone?

ABBY: I do.

ASHLEY: Of course you do.

(TRACY *follows* ABBY *to her C D player and puts in the C D.* SAMANTHA's *singing voice is recorded on the C D. The lyrics can be sung to an original tune or to Disney's* A Whole New World *or ANY tune of preference. The lyrics can also be adjusted to fit a tune.* ABBY, TRACY, *and* ZOE *go in and out of hysterical laughter while shushing each other so they can hear.* ASHLEY *awkwardly pretends not to care as* ABBY *takes a victory.)*

SAMANTHA:
Please share in my joy
On a special day
In my life
When I become a Bat Mitzvah.
Saturday, the twenty-fifth of September
Two thousand and nine at ten o'clock in the morning
Congregation Temple Israel!

Oh, join us! Please join us!
I'll see you there!

ABBY: We should play it again!

TRACY/ZOE: Yeah! Play it!

TRACY: If I had a good voice, I would totally sing my invitation.

ASHLEY: Well, it's a good thing you don't sing, cause then we wouldn't be friends with you.

ABBY: I'd be friends with you.

ZOE: I'd be friends with you so you can be like my personal radio.

ABBY: Ashley could be a personal radio because she sings pop.

ZOE: Yeah, but Samantha's better.

(TRACY *plays the C D again.* ABBY, TRACY, *and* ZOE *attempt to sing along obnoxiously while continuing with the shaving cream.* ASHLEY *holds her moshi pillow to her chest.*)

ABBY: Do the tickle thing on her face!

TRACY/ZOE: Yeah!

(ABBY *applies shaving cream to* SAMANTHA*'s palm.* ZOE *grabs* ABBY*'s hair without her permission to tickle* SAMANTHA*'s face.* SAMANTHA *swats her face, opens her eyes, and screams. Her C D is still playing.*)

SAMANTHA: Ahh! What is this? Ow! My eye!

ABBY/ZOE: Surprise!

TRACY: Surprise jack attack!

SAMANTHA: Ow, my eye is burning. Fuck!

TRACY: Oh, no!

SAMANTHA: It hurts!

ABBY: You shouldn't have fallen asleep.

ASHLEY: You are such a fucking bitch, Abby.

ABBY: What?

SAMANTHA: Is that my C D? Turn it off. Turn it off!

TRACY: O K, it's off, it's off. Here.

ASHLEY: Samantha, are you O K? Abby thought it would be funny to rip your Jonas Brothers poster down for no reason. And then she stole your invitation and made us all play it so we'd like her. Oh, and then she put shaving cream in your eye.

ABBY: Not on purpose!

ZOE: Yeah, you did!

TRACY: Um, here's water.

SAMANTHA: My eye!

ABBY: Calm down! I'm sorry. I didn't mean to.

TRACY: Here's a towel.

SAMANTHA: Ow.

TRACY: I'm so sorry. It was supposed to be a joke.

SAMANTHA: Ow. I was sleeping, god. Ow!

ABBY: We're sorry, we said.

SAMANTHA: No, you're not.

ABBY: Well, how many times do we have to say it?

SAMANTHA: Why would you do this?

TRACY: I don't know. We were kidding. We thought it would be funny.

SAMANTHA: It's everywhere. Oh my god.

ABBY: Write it on your personal list if you're so upset.

SAMANTHA: I can't even see yet!

TRACY: Well, it doesn't stain. I'll help you get it off.

ABBY: Yeah, Ashley said it doesn't stain so you'll be fine.

ASHLEY: It doesn't.

SAMANTHA: Yeah, but it's all over my clothes!

TRACY: You can borrow mine until laundry day.

SAMANTHA: Yeah, right. I'm not touching your clothes.

TRACY: Fine. I was just trying to be nice.

SAMANTHA: Well, you can all go to hell!

ASHLEY: Ooh. Hell.

SAMANTHA: I hope you all fucking die!

ASHLEY: Ooh. Death.

TRACY: Seriously?

(SAMANTHA *storms off into the bathroom to clean up.* TRACY *goes to help her.*)

ASHLEY: Well, I think it's time.

ZOE: For what?

ASHLEY: Everyone put on all black.

ABBY: Why?

ZOE: A raid!

ABBY: A raid?

ZOE: I'm hooking up! I'm hooking up!

(ABBY, ASHLEY, *and* ZOE *throw black clothes on and apply dark smudges under their eyes with black eye-shadow.*)

ABBY: Flashlights!

ZOE: I need one. Give me yours!

ABBY: Mine?

ZOE: Yeah. Thanks!

ABBY: Are we going right now?

ZOE: I'm scared!

(ASHLEY *turns the lights out.*)

ABBY: I can't see anything.

ASHLEY: Everyone turn your flashlights on.

ABBY: I don't have a flashlight now.

(SAMANTHA *and* TRACY *enter from the bathroom, holding hands.* TRACY *turns the lights back on.*)

TRACY: Woah, what's going on?

ASHLEY: Shh.

TRACY: Are we going on a raid?

ABBY: Yeah!

TRACY: Yes!

ASHLEY: Samantha, are you excited?

SAMANTHA: I'm not talking to any of you except Tracy.

ABBY: Your loss. We're all gonna hook up tonight!

ZOE: No, I'm hooking up! This is my night, not yours.

ASHLEY: Abby, who in this camp is going to hook up with you?

ABBY: I don't know. Like a lot of people.

SAMANTHA: Are you going to limp there?

ABBY: My ankle feels better, thank you very much. And now that I just hooked up with Zoe, I know how to do everything.

ASHLEY: You're kidding, right?

ABBY: No, I mean, it can't be that hard. You've been doing it forever.

TRACY: What?

ZOE: Who forever?

ASHLEY: Yeah, Abby, who forever?

ABBY: What?

ASHLEY: Say it.

ABBY: What? Oh, I'm not like telling on you.

ASHLEY: What would you tell, Abby?

ABBY: Nothing.

ZOE: You're being annoying.

ASHLEY: No, it's fine. Say it.

ABBY: Wait, what?

ASHLEY: I dare you.

ABBY: I'm confused.

ASHLEY: Abby, have you ever had an orgasm?

ABBY: No. I don't think so.

ASHLEY: You don't think so?

ABBY: I mean, probably not.

ASHLEY: I mean, do you know what it feels like?

ABBY: Yeah. I guess.

ASHLEY: No, you don't. Have you ever seen a penis?

ABBY: No, but I know—

ASHLEY: Have you ever had anything shoved up your vagina?

ABBY: I don't know.

ASHLEY: What do you mean you don't know?

ABBY: I don't know. You're confusing me.

ASHLEY: Well, have you or haven't you?

ABBY: No. Wait, like up there?

ASHLEY: Yes, up there.

ABBY: Um, up the vagina?

ASHLEY: Abby, what do you know about sex?

ABBY: Like a lot.

ASHLEY: Well, go. We'd all like to hear what you know.

ABBY: Like sex stuff.

ASHLEY: More.

ABBY: Um, spitting versus swallowing.

ASHLEY: Boring.

ABBY: Um, doggie style versus regular way or something.

ASHLEY: It's called missionary, Abby. Missionary.

ABBY: Oh, yeah.

ASHLEY: Oh, yeah, what?

ABBY: I don't know.

ASHLEY: You don't know?

ABBY: Yeah.

ASHLEY: You don't know WHAT?

ABBY: I don't know. Stop talking!

ASHLEY: You know what I think?

ABBY: No.

ASHLEY: I think you are a dumb, innocent, fat girl who has never really hooked up, never had a boy like her.

ABBY: That's not true!

ASHLEY: You wake up and your mom makes you heart-shaped french toast before school. And that's the only love you'll ever get.

ABBY: No, I will, Ashley. I will get love!

ASHLEY: Do you think your dad loves you?

ABBY: Not the way your dad loves you.

ASHLEY: O K.

ABBY: No, I don't... That's not what I meant—

ASHLEY: You wanna talk about family? Let's talk.

(ASHLEY *flicks the lights back on.*)

ASHLEY: We know that Tracy's mom smokes pot and likes to vacuum the house completely naked.

TRACY: She always assumes no one's home.

ZOE: I saw her butt once!

ASHLEY: We know that Zoe's sister was on iCarly cause her mom did it with her agent.

ZOE: I said they went out on a date.

(ASHLEY *earmuffs* ZOE.)

ASHLEY: They fucked. (*She releases the earmuffs.*) We know that Samantha's mom is screwing…

ZOE: Boom, boom, boom!

ASHLEY: Your dad.

ABBY: Shut up!

ASHLEY: Exactly. YOU shut up! SHUT THE FUCK UP!

ABBY: It's not his fault! It's your mom's fault, Samantha!

SAMANTHA: Why are you talking to me?

ABBY: Why does she have to be my dad's secretary and why does she have to be such a slut?

SAMANTHA: She's not! And stop talking about it! My dad doesn't even know about our parents and all of you do cause of your big mouth, Abby!

ABBY: Well, maybe if he knew, he wouldn't let your slut mom cheat on him!

TRACY: Um, he probably knows, Samantha.

SAMANTHA: He can't know! Then he'll divorce my mom. He can't know!

ABBY: How can he not know? Is he retarded? My mom knows! We ALL know.

ZOE: Yeah, he probably knows.

SAMANTHA: He's not retarded!

ABBY: They're gonna get a divorce anyway.

SAMANTHA: No! Then I won't see him ever.

ABBY: Then you'll know how it feels! He was supposed to go to Puerto Rico with our family but instead he took YOU to a Hannah Montana concert!

SAMANTHA: I didn't want to go with him. I don't even like your dad. I just wanted to go to the concert.

ABBY: Well, I love my dad and I wanted to go my whole life! I should have gone with my dad, NOT YOU!

SAMANTHA: Well, tell HIM that, not me!

ABBY: I did. I said, "Dad, I'm twelve. I'm not five. I know you're not just working. I know you're going to a hotel to have an affair with a slut! And I love Hannah Montana!"

ZOE: That sucks, Abby, but lots of fathers cheat with other people and stuff.

ABBY: You've ruined my life!

ZOE: You're not special.

SAMANTHA: You think I want to invite you to my Bat Mitzvah? You think I want to be here so we can be like best friends?

ZOE: I can't wait till you're sisters.

ABBY: Fine. Go home. Zoe, where's your cell phone?

TRACY: You have your cell phone here?

ZOE: Abby, you weren't supposed to tell anyone!

TRACY: We all had to give in our cell phones on the first day.

SAMANTHA: I saw you give yours in.

ZOE: I brought two.

ABBY: We're calling your dad, Samantha.

ZOE: Yes!

SAMANTHA: No, you're not.

ZOE: Oh my god. Oh my god.

SAMANTHA: You don't even have my number.

ZOE: Yes, I do! I have EVERYONE's number!

ABBY: Give me your phone, Zoe.

(ZOE *fishes out her phone from deep within her lockbox under her bed, turns it on, and gives it to* ABBY.)

SAMANTHA: Don't you dare!

ABBY: Ready?

SAMANTHA: STOP IT!

ABBY: Now you get to go home! Isn't that what you want? You're a bitch to everyone anyway!

ZOE: Beyotch!

ABBY: Now your parents will get a divorce and you'll lose your dad and know what it feels like and then I'm going to beg my dad to come back and we'll never be sisters ever, ever, ever which is good cause you're a slut just like your mom!

SAMANTHA: Stop calling her a slut!

ABBY: Slut, slut, slut!

SAMANTHA: Stop it!

ABBY: You took my dad from me. You have two dads and I have none.

SAMANTHA: Well, you can take your dad back. I said I hate him! Are you deaf?

ABBY: I'm calling in three, two...

ZOE: There's no service there. You have to go to the third toilet.

ABBY: Fine! Three, two...

ZOE: Stand on it, close to the window.

(ABBY *races to the bathroom.* SAMANTHA *runs after her.*)

SAMANTHA: Give it to me!

ABBY: Never, never, never!

SAMANTHA: Now!

ABBY: No, I said!

SAMANTHA: Stop it, I'm serious!

ABBY: Ow, let go!

SAMANTHA: No, you let go!

ABBY: No, you!

SAMANTHA: You're gonna—

ABBY: You idiot!

SAMANTHA: You're the one who dropped it!

ZOE: What?

TRACY: Oh, no.

ABBY: I wasn't going to call!

ZOE: You dropped my phone?

SAMANTHA: Yeah, right.

TRACY: Uh-oh, spaghettio.

SAMANTHA: Get it out of the toilet!

TRACY: It's in the toilet?

ZOE: Wait, it's in the toilet?

(TRACY *and* ZOE *run into the bathroom.* ASHLEY *is left alone. ALONE. She is stewing with resentment.*)

ABBY: Just, I could kill you I hate you so much!

SAMANTHA: I hate it here and I hate all of you!

ZOE: My phone! My mom's gonna kill me!

ABBY: Go to hell!

(ABBY *runs back into the bunk followed by all the girls, grabs* SAMANTHA's *C D, and smashes it into pieces with a shaving cream bottle.*)

TRACY: Wow, Abby. Real mature!

ZOE: Rudeness!

TRACY: That was like the meanest thing you could have done, Abby!

ZOE: Even I wouldn't break her singing.

TRACY: Her C D, Zoe, her C D.

ZOE: Like, I can be mean sometimes, but not that mean.

ASHLEY: Abby's a selfish bitch. She can't help herself. It happens.

TRACY: Apologize to Samantha!

ZOE: Yeah, say you're sorry!

TRACY: Say it.

ASHLEY: What are you waiting for?

ZOE: Yeah, what are you waiting for?

TRACY: Abby, come on!

ZOE: Just say it.

TRACY: Say I'm sorry.

ASHLEY: Oh my god, are you kidding?

TRACY: Come on!

ZOE: Go!

TRACY: Seriously?

ASHLEY: Abby!

ZOE: Abby!

TRACY: Abby!

ZOE: You start every fight in this bunk.

TRACY: Come on, Abby!

ASHLEY: Say it now.

ZOE: Come on, rude-face!

TRACY: Say it!

ASHLEY: Now.

ZOE: Now.

TRACY: Go!

ZOE: What's the matter, Abby?

TRACY: Hello?

ASHLEY: Abby's gone retarded and can't speak.

TRACY/ZOE: Abby!

(SAMANTHA *storms toward the door to get Christy. She is done. Game over. As soon as she reaches the door,* ABBY *projectile vomits.* SAMANTHA *turns around. Silence)*

ZOE: Um, Abby just threw up.

TRACY: O K, wow, Zoe, get her a bag or something.

ZOE: Oh my god, oh my god.

TRACY: Someone get her water.

ZOE: Ew, so gross. So gross.

TRACY: Ash, get her water.

(ASHLEY *is videotaping and does not move or answer.* SAMANTHA *gets* ABBY *some water and hands it off to* TRACY.)

TRACY: Thanks. Are you O K, Abby?

ABBY: Um, I don't know. Ew, ew, ew.

TRACY: It's O K, Abby.

ABBY: No, it's not. Yuck. Ew.

ZOE: Your hair has puke in it.

(SAMANTHA *takes a step away from the door, removes her hair tie from her wrist, and hands it to* TRACY. TRACY *ties* ABBY's *hair back.)*

TRACY: Thanks.

ABBY: Ew, ew, ew, ew.

ZOE: Are you done throwing up?

ABBY: Ew, ew, ew, ew, ew, ew.

TRACY: You're fine, Abby. It's O K.

ABBY: Ew. It's so nasty.

TRACY: Stop freaking out.

ZOE: You're making me nauseous.

ABBY: I'm not freaking out!

ZOE: Yes, you are.

TRACY: It's alright, Abby. Calm down.

ABBY: I think I'm done. I don't know. Ew.

ZOE: Are you sure?

TRACY: You're done?

ABBY: I think so.

TRACY: You think so or you are?

ABBY: I don't know. It just comes out. How do I know?

ZOE: Just don't like go near my stuff.

ABBY: Is it really in my hair?

ZOE: I wasn't lying.

TRACY: Here. O K, I'm getting it out.

ABBY: Ew, so gross.

TRACY: I can't believe I'm touching your vomit.

ZOE: Sick.

(TRACY *runs off to the bathroom to wash her hands. Pause.*
SAMANTHA *turns back toward the door, hesitates, turns
back toward* ABBY.)

SAMANTHA: Sorry.

(ABBY *is silent.* ASHLEY *zooms in on* ABBY. ABBY *is very
aware that she is on camera. She checks in with the camera
self-consciously as she and* SAMANTHA *go at it. She is*

ASHLEY's *puppet and responds to* SAMANTHA *how she imagines* ASHLEY *wants her to.)*

SAMANTHA: Like, I don't think we should fight anymore.

(ABBY *is silent.)*

SAMANTHA: Cause it's dumb and whatever's done is done.

ABBY: O K.

SAMANTHA: Like, if I have to be here and you have to be here, we should try to get along or whatever, cause it'll be a long summer if we don't.

ABBY: What are you talking about?

SAMANTHA: What don't you get?

ABBY: Why would I want to get along with you?

SAMANTHA: What?

ABBY: I want it to be a long summer. I love camp.

SAMANTHA: Riiight.

ABBY: What is that supposed to mean?

SAMANTHA: You can say that, but I mean, everyone's mean to you. So…

ASHLEY: Who's mean to her?

ZOE: Yeah, who's mean to her?

ABBY: Yeah, I mean, sorry, but who's mean to me?

SAMANTHA: I'm just saying people are mean to you and I'll be nice from now on. That's it.

(SAMANTHA *goes toward the door.)*

ZOE: We're not mean to her. You are.

ASHLEY: Abby's our best friend.

ZOE: Like bestest bestest friend. We hate YOU for being such a bitch to her.

SAMANTHA: *(Stopping to answer)* Forget it. I was trying to be nice.

(SAMANTHA *takes another step toward the door.* ASHLEY *advances toward* SAMANTHA *with the camera rolling.)*

ASHLEY: We love Abby.

ZOE: And we hate you.

ABBY: And I love Zoe and Ashley like sisters.

ASHLEY: Sisters.

SAMANTHA: O K, I get it. Best friends. Sisters.

(SAMANTHA *walks toward the door again.* ASHLEY *steps in front of her, blocking her way, camera still rolling.)*

SAMANTHA: Move.

ASHLEY: But then you had to come…

ZOE: And like pretend to be her sister or something.

SAMANTHA: I never pretended…you are all clearly too immature to see that I was apologi—

ABBY: I LOVE it here.

ASHLEY: Abby LOVES it here.

ZOE: She LOVES it here.

SAMANTHA: Oh yeah, now that you just said it three times, I totally see that!

ABBY: I do!

ASHLEY/ZOE: She does.

ABBY: If you hate camp so much because you're not friends with me and Ashley and Zoe, and you like feel left out, then go home.

SAMANTHA: Are you serious?

ASHLEY: Very serious.

SAMANTHA: Ashley HATES you. It's so obvious.

ABBY: Obviously not if you were listening to what she was saying about me!

SAMANTHA: They both make fun of you all the time. Are you insane?

ABBY: You probably make fun of me behind my back. At least some people have the decency to do it to my face.

SAMANTHA: That's pathetic. I just feel bad for you now.

ABBY: Wanna know what's pathetic? Being at a camp where no one likes you, everyone thinks you're a loser, and wants you to go home and never come back!

SAMANTHA: I don't give a shit what people think about me because I know I'm more mature than all of you, and I don't need to like suck up to whoever's popular.

ZOE: Did you just call me popular?

ABBY: I don't suck up!

SAMANTHA: Yes, you do.

ABBY: I don't have to suck up to anyone! You do cause you have no friends to suck up to!

SAMANTHA: You're not even making any sense.

ABBY: Does this make sense: were you dissing my best friends, yes or no?

SAMANTHA: They're NOT your friends.

ASHLEY: She is.

ZOE: Our best friend.

ABBY: See? I said, were you dissing my best friends?

SAMANTHA: Maybe I was, Abby. What are you gonna do about it? Throw up some more?

ABBY: You jealous shit whore slut dad-stealer stupid idiot!

SAMANTHA: *(Chuckling)* Is that really the best you can do?

(ASHLEY *is still videotaping and loving it.)*

ASHLEY: Oh shit! This is good. This is really good.

ZOE: *(Singing)* So good, uh-uh…

ASHLEY: Answer her question, Abby.

ABBY: What question?

ASHLEY: Are you going to just let Samantha be mean to your best friends?

ABBY: No!

ZOE: Are you just gonna let her say we're popular and awesome?

ABBY: No! I mean, yes. Wait, what?

ASHLEY: Or are you gonna throw up more?

ABBY: Maybe I will throw up. On YOU, Samantha!

ZOE: Ha! Ha! Gross!

ASHLEY: Come on, Abby. You're boring me. What are you going to do?

SAMANTHA: Yeah, Abby, what are you going to do?

ABBY: Something bad. Don't worry.

SAMANTHA: O K, have fun.

ABBY: Fine. I will.

SAMANTHA: Cause I'm really scared in case you can't tell.

ZOE: Diss!

ASHLEY: We defended you.

ZOE: It's true.

ASHLEY: We'd do anything for you. Prove your friendship.

ZOE: Stand up for us!

ASHLEY: Do something!

ABBY: I am.

ASHLEY: We're waiting.

ZOE: Show her who's boss!

ASHLEY: Oh my god, Zoe, you are so cute!

ZOE: No, you are!

ASHLEY: Abby, go!

ZOE: Christy's coming in soon. Come on!

ABBY: What? I'm thinking.

ASHLEY: Go!

ABBY: What do you want from me? I just threw up!

ZOE: Get over it.

ASHLEY: If Christy comes in before you stand up for us…

ABBY: What do you want me to do?

ASHLEY: Zoe, say good-bye to Abby.

ZOE: Good-bye, vomit-face!

ABBY: Wait, what're you doing?

ASHLEY: You're dead to me in five—

ABBY: Wait, no, wait!

ASHLEY: Four—

ABBY: No!

ASHLEY: Three—

ABBY: O K, O K, I'll do something.

ASHLEY: Two—

ABBY: Stop! O K!

ASHLEY: Aaaand—

(ABBY *rushes to* SAMANTHA's *pillow, pulls out her diary from her pillowcase, and opens it to a very specific page. It is clear that* ABBY *has read* SAMANTHA's *diary before.* SAMANTHA *goes to stop her.* ASHLEY *pulls* SAMANTHA's *hair to restrain her.* SAMANTHA *struggles.*)

SAMANTHA: Abby, stop! Don't touch my things. Stop!

ASHLEY: Woah, Abby. Bringing out the bitch. Love it.

SAMANTHA: Don't do it! Get off of me!

ASHLEY: Yes, Abby, yes.

ZOE: Her diary! Hidden!

SAMANTHA: Stop it! Abby, stop it right now!

ZOE: Oh my god!

SAMANTHA: STOP! Ashley, you are hurting me!!!

ZOE: Read it, Abby, read it!

(SAMANTHA *continues struggling with* ASHLEY. *She succumbs to mortified tears as* ABBY *reads aloud her diary entry.*)

ABBY: "May 21, 2009.
10:07 P M.
Oh my god. Tonight I had my first kiss with Lily. I was really scared at first because I've like never kissed a girl before. Only guys. It's not really that different. But it kind of is. Lily used a little bit of tongue and when Ben and I kissed he was darting his tongue and it was kind of gross. So Lily was less gross slash not gross at all but also she's like my best friend and we know each other really well so it makes sense that the kiss was good cause we get it. Like she has really soft lips and is really pretty and stuff. And Ben has chapped lips and is kind of dumb. I'm really happy. It might happen again tomorrow cause we have a sleepover."
And now a poem.

ZOE: You wrote a poem about it?

ASHLEY: Abby, keep going!

(TRACY *enters from the bathroom.*)

ABBY: "Her eyes catch mine
Our legs touch in her bed
We laugh at each other and know
We know"

TRACY: Ashley, let go of her.

ASHLEY: Oh my god.

ABBY: "I close my eyes and feel the kiss"

TRACY: Are you kidding? Let go of her! Abby, what are you reading?

ABBY: "The moonlight comes through the window"

TRACY: Seriously, stop it!

ASHLEY: This is, wow, this is…

ABBY: "The magic of the night
My heart skips a beat
Thumping, thumping, stopped"

(TRACY *tries to grab the diary out of* ABBY's *hand.* ABBY *tears the page out, throws the diary at* TRACY, *runs away, and continues to read aloud, standing on top of* ASHLEY's *bed.* TRACY *chases her around the bunk and then goes to* ASHLEY.)

TRACY: Ashley, let her go. What the fuck?

ABBY: "We breathe together
Best friends
And more."

(ASHLEY *throws* SAMANTHA *to the floor.* ASHLEY *and* ZOE *laugh hysterically.*)

ASHLEY: And more. Wow.

ZOE: Wow!

ASHLEY: Oh my god!

TRACY: Are you O K?

ZOE: We were right. She is a lesbian!

ASHLEY: Oh my god!

TRACY: It's O K, Samantha. It's O K.

(TRACY *attempts to comfort* SAMANTHA *who stays paralyzed on the floor.*)

ZOE: Like we were kidding before but now it's real life!

ASHLEY: I know! Holy shit!

ZOE: What the what!

SAMANTHA: It's none of your business! I hate hate hate all of you!

TRACY: Alright. It's O K, it's O K.

SAMANTHA: It's not O K! You're the only one who's nice in this bunk and I'm sorry I was a bitch to you before, but how are you friends with them?

TRACY: Calm down. It's O K.

ZOE: Actually Tracy loves us. Right, Tracy?

TRACY: It's O K. Stop crying.

ZOE: Leave her, Tracy. She said she hates us!

TRACY: Come on, Samantha. Let's go.

ZOE: Tracy! Hello? Tracy!

TRACY: You O K? We'll clean you up.

SAMANTHA: My head.

ZOE: Tracy! I'm talking to you!

TRACY: Ashley has Advil hidden somewhere.

ABBY: Oh my GOD!

ZOE: What?

ABBY: They're gonna kiss! They're gonna make out! Oh my god! They're girlfriends!

ZOE: Haha! No! Really?

ABBY: Yeah!

ZOE: Oh my god!

(TRACY *ignores them and starts to head to the bathroom with* SAMANTHA.)

ABBY: You should have just stayed in the bathroom.

TRACY: Oh, right. Cause it's not like I was in there to get your vomit out from under my fingernails or anything.

ZOE: Ew.

ABBY: I never asked for your help.

ZOE: She didn't.

TRACY: Ashley, where's your Advil?

ABBY: Don't give it to her!

ZOE: Yeah, don't! She's a traitor!

ABBY/ZOE: Traitor!

(TRACY *ignores* ABBY *and* ZOE *and waits for an answer from* ASHLEY. ASHLEY *is conflicted and so says nothing.* TRACY *stands in* ASHLEY'*s face, waiting.*)

ASHLEY: You're too close to me. Move.

TRACY: I'm waiting.

ASHLEY: Move!

TRACY: Are you getting your Advil or not?

ASHLEY: Get out of my face!

TRACY: No.

ASHLEY: What the fuck is your problem?

TRACY: Samantha has a headache because you were pulling her hair.

ASHLEY: Who cares.

TRACY: Advil.

ASHLEY: Get out of my personal space.

TRACY: No. Get your Advil.

ASHLEY: Move!

TRACY: Where do you hide it?

ASHLEY: Move!

TRACY: No!

ASHLEY: Move, I said. Move!

TRACY: Not until you—

(ASHLEY *slaps* TRACY *across the face. Silence*)

ASHLEY: What?

(TRACY *gives her a silent stare-down.* ASHLEY *pauses briefly between each of the following lines as she struggles to defend herself and stay on top.*)

ASHLEY: Whatever, it's not my fault.
You were in my way.
Stop staring at me all weird.
I'm not scared of you.

TRACY: You should be.

ASHLEY: Chill out, Tracy.

TRACY: Don't talk. Don't look at me.

ASHLEY: It was a joke!

TRACY: It's just a matter of time before you lose all your friends. We'll find the Advil on our own, you bitch.

(TRACY *and* SAMANTHA *reach the bathroom door.* TRACY *turns around.*)

TRACY: Oh, I almost forgot. Ryan told me that when he fingered you, you cried. Like a baby.

(TRACY *exits with* SAMANTHA *to the bathroom.*)

ZOE: You cried?

ABBY: Why did you cry?

ZOE: That's so awkward!

ABBY: You said it doesn't hurt!

ZOE: You lied?

ABBY: Aw, Ashley! I think it's cute you cried!

ZOE: Ryan probably didn't think it was cute.

ABBY: Well, it doesn't matter. Ryan's dumb.

ZOE: What if she did lose all her friends?

ABBY: That would be so weird.

ZOE: I can't even picture it!

(ABBY *hugs* ASHLEY. ASHLEY *has a visceral reaction.*)

ABBY: Don't worry, I'll be your best friend no matter what you do! Even if you cry.

ASHLEY: Get off.

(ABBY *still hugs* ASHLEY.)

ABBY: I'm not perfect. You're not perfect. And we both have problems with our dads!

(ASHLEY *snaps, ripping* ABBY *off of her.*)

ASHLEY: Oh my god, I never thought you were perfect! Why would anyone EVER think you're perfect?

ZOE: Yeah, you're not perfect.

ASHLEY: Your mom is fugly. Fuckin ugly. Disaster. And you still don't know anything about what it means to be a woman. Obviously your mom couldn't teach you very much cause she couldn't hold on to a strong man like your dad.

ABBY: She could!

ASHLEY: He's gone, Abby. Forever.

ABBY: That's not true!

ASHLEY: He's forgetting you right now.

ABBY: No, he's not!

ASHLEY: You'll never learn how to be a woman.

ABBY: I will!

ASHLEY: No guy is ever going to be with you, and then if he finally is, he's gonna leave you just like your dad left your mom!

ABBY: Stop saying that.

ASHLEY: And never come back!

ABBY: He's gonna come back and she'll hold on to him and I'll know what being a woman is and I am almost a woman now so shut up!

ASHLEY: Abby, lie down. We are going to perform a séance on you.

ZOE: Why not me?

ABBY: Really?

ASHLEY: Because, Zoe, you're too cute.

ZOE: What does that have to do with it?

ASHLEY: You're hooking up with Jason tonight.

ZOE: Jake.

ASHLEY: Jake. Whatever. You'll get experience later. Abby needs to become a woman now cause no guy is going to want to hook up with her until she's pretty.

ZOE: She's prettyish.

ASHLEY: Don't falsely feed her ego.

ZOE: If she weren't so fat. Remember also that time when I fed you an eggo—

(ASHLEY *suddenly screams.*)

ASHLEY: Did that scare you, Abby?

ABBY: No.

ASHLEY: Well, then you're ready to be initiated to the other world. Where heaven and hell dance a dance of doom! This séance will release you from your innocence!

ZOE: I want to be the victim! I want to be the victim!

ASHLEY: No, Abby needs to be the victim. Her sexuality needs to emerge. I said, you'll hook up later.

ABBY: Yeah, Zoe. You'll hook up later.

ASHLEY: Abby needs to learn what being a woman is all about.

ABBY: Yeah, I need to learn what being a woman is all about.

ZOE: You're copying her.

ASHLEY: Lie down on the bed.

ABBY: O K.

ZOE: What do I do?

ASHLEY: O K. Zoe, sit on her vagina and pin her arms down.

ZOE: Like this?

ASHLEY: But really strong.

ZOE: This is weird.

ABBY: Just do it.

ASHLEY: Where's the duct tape?

ABBY: Why?

ASHLEY: Zoe, where's the duct tape?

ZOE: It's not mine.

ASHLEY: I don't care. Where is it?

ZOE: I don't know.

ABBY: Ow, Zoe, you're on my stomach.

ZOE: I don't want to do this.

ABBY: Stop being so jealous.

ZOE: Ew, I'm not.

(ASHLEY *tapes* ABBY's *wrists to the headboard of the bed.*
ABBY *tries to say something, but no one can understand her.*
ASHLEY *tapes* ABBY's *legs around the bed.*)

ZOE: Do I just stay here?

ASHLEY: Yeah.

ZOE: I want to video her!

ASHLEY: No.

ZOE: I want to, though!

ASHLEY: Fine. Ten seconds.

(ASHLEY *hastily snatches* ZOE's *camera and videotapes her.*)

ZOE: Are you videotaping me now?

ASHLEY: Yeah. Go.

ZOE: Wait, put it on a funny setting!

ASHLEY: Go.

ZOE: I am Zoe. And this is Abby! She destroyed my
phone. We are about to do the séance. Sometimes we
bring people back from the dead. Like our grandmas
and stuff. Are you scared, Abby? She's not saying
anything. Right, she can't talk. The tape on her mouth.
Shhh. Abby, stop! You sound scary! O K, what, you
wanna say something? Do you? O K, say vagina.
What? I can't hear you! I don't get what she's saying.
I think she said big fat penis. O K, wait, what else do I
say? Oh, and this is my sexy, sexy face. And this is my
sexy body. Zoom in on my cleavage!

ASHLEY: O K, we're done.

ZOE: Did you get my boob?

ASHLEY: Keep her down on the bed.

ZOE: Is that part going to be in the documentary?

ASHLEY: Don't move, Zoe.

ZOE: I'm not, but she's like staring at me. Abby, stop staring at me.

ASHLEY: It's fine.

ZOE: I can't look at her.

ASHLEY: Put this over her face.

(ASHLEY *hands her a pink towel drooping over the side of the bed, and* ZOE *drops it on* ABBY's *face.*)

ASHLEY: Now the séance may begin.

(ASHLEY *turns the lights off.* ABBY *is still.*)

ASHLEY: You are twelve years old, very innocent, like a rose. You exude innocence and rosiness. People say you're fat. But it's just baby fat. Cause you are a baby. You dream of someone sticking his dick in your vagina. You dream of it. You might want me to do it. But that's not possible. Cause I don't have a dick. Thank god. Then I'd be weird. But you hope that someone big and strong like your dad will come and do this. You want to be raped.

ZOE: No one wants to be raped.

ASHLEY: Yeah, well, you don't know anything about it Zoe…so shut up! Abby, you want to be raped cause then you don't have to make the effort. It will just come to you. The day will come, Abigail Sarah Sullner. Some day, your innocence will be plucked. Like a rose.

(ZOE *puts a pillow on* ABBY's *face and then sits on it to watch* ASHLEY *as she speaks.* ABBY *can't breathe, and struggles, but neither of them notices. She eventually vomits and chokes.*)

ASHLEY: It always comes back to the rose. And when it does, your vagina will grow lots of curly hairs and

you will lose your stomach and you will blossom. And
your dad will be proud like mine. He'll love you so
much. And your best friends, Zoe and I, will be there.
To congratulate you. We'll give you presents but the
best present will be the dick that was inside you. And
you won't get pregnant. Don't worry. Cause you will
be changing from baby-hood to woman-hood. You are
almost a teenager, Abigail Sarah Sullner. But not for
long. You will soon be a woman!

(ASHLEY *pulls down* ABBY's *pajama pants. She writes, "I
WAS RAPED" on her thigh with pink lipstick and reads it
out loud while scribbling.* ASHLEY *notices that* ABBY *is still.
She looks at* ZOE *who is still sitting on* ABBY's *face, looking
at* ASHLEY *in awe of her actions.*)

ZOE: I want to write something! Let me!

ASHLEY: Wait, why are you sitting on her face?

ZOE: I want to draw squiggly lines on her vagina!

ASHLEY: Get up!

ZOE: What?

ASHLEY: Zoe, get up!

(ASHLEY *shoves* ZOE *off the bed, flicks on the lights, and
stares at* ABBY's *still body. After a few seconds,* ASHLEY
snatches the pink towel off ABBY's *face.*)

ZOE: Oh my God, Abby. Stop it.

ASHLEY: Abby, wake up!

ZOE: She's such a faker!

ASHLEY: Abby, get up!

(ASHLEY *tries to undo the tape manually but struggles.
After a few seconds of unsuccessful maneuvering, she
makes her way to the counselor's area and grabs a pair of
scissors. She starts cutting the duct tape with animalistic
ferociousness and fear.* ZOE *stands against the wall, staring*

blankly. ASHLEY *removes the tape from* ABBY's *mouth. Vomit.* ABBY *is still.)*

ZOE: She'll be fine.

ASHLEY: She just passed out.

ZOE: Yeah, she just passed out.

ASHLEY: Oh my god, I didn't even finish the séance. I mean, I didn't even do anything.

ZOE: It's not like you actually raped her.

ASHLEY: You don't die from being raped.

ZOE: I know. But, like, you didn't rape her.

ASHLEY: We were totally kidding.

ZOE: You were just trying to help her.

ASHLEY: You were trying to help her too.

ZOE: No.

ASHLEY: Yeah, you were.

ZOE: I didn't know what you were doing. I was helping you.

ASHLEY: Oh my god, Zoe. That's so mean. You weren't trying to help Abby?

ZOE: That's not what I meant.

ASHLEY: You just said you didn't want to help her. You wanted to hurt her. Why would you want to do that?

ZOE: That's not it!

ASHLEY: I can't believe you. I'm sorry.

ZOE: I'm so confused!

ASHLEY: Me too. I thought you were my friend.

ZOE: I am!

ASHLEY: Well, my friends don't kill people. They especially don't kill my best friend.

ZOE: I didn't! I didn't!

ASHLEY: I saw you put the towel over her.

ZOE: You're just mad cause your dad rapes you!

(Silence)

ASHLEY: I'm going to get the counselors. I'm telling them all what you've done. It's O K, Zoe. Everyone makes mistakes. This is just a really bad one.

(ASHLEY grabs ZOE's camera and takes a picture of ZOE next to ABBY's dead body. She exits through the front door, to the porch. ZOE is left alone. She takes ASHLEY's moshi pillow and tries to suffocate herself. She runs out of breath and removes the pillow. She stands staring into space, empty, defeated, and lost.)

END OF PLAY